Magit 2.1 Reference Manual

A catalogue record for this book is available from the Hong Kong Public Libraries.

Published by Samurai Media Limited.

Email: info@samuraimedia.org

ISBN 978-988-14435-0-2

Table of Contents

1 Introduction

Magit is an interface to the version control system Git, implemented as an Emacs package. Magit aspires to be a complete Git porcelain. While we cannot (yet) claim that Magit wraps and improves upon each and every Git command, it is complete enough to allow even experienced Git users to perform almost all of their daily version control tasks directly from within Emacs. While many fine Git clients exist, only Magit and Git itself deserve to be called porcelains.

Staging and otherwise applying changes is one of the most important features in a Git porcelain and here Magit outshines anything else, including Git itself. Git's own staging interface (`git add --patch`) is so cumbersome that many users only use it in exceptional cases. In Magit staging a hunk or even just part of a hunk is as trivial as staging all changes made to a file.

The most visible part of Magit's interface is the status buffer, which displays information about the current repository. Its content is created by running several Git commands and making their output actionable. Among other things, it displays information about the current branch, lists unpulled and unpushed changes and contains sections displaying the staged and unstaged changes. That might sound noisy, but, since sections are collapsible, it's not.

To stage or unstage a change one places the cursor on the change and then types `s` or `u`. The change can be a file or a hunk, or when the region is active (i.e. when there is a selection) several files or hunks, or even just part of a hunk. The change or changes that these commands - and many others - would act on are highlighted.

Magit also implements several other "apply variants" in addition to staging and unstaging. One can discard or reverse a change, or apply it to the working tree. Git's own porcelain only supports this for staging and unstaging and you would have to do something like `git diff ... | ??? | git apply ...` to discard, revert, or apply a single hunk on the command line. In fact that's exactly what Magit does internally (which is what lead to the term "apply variants").

Magit isn't just for Git experts, but it does assume some prior experience with Git as well as Emacs. That being said, many users have reported that using Magit was what finally taught them what Git it is capable off and how to use it to its fullest. Other users wished they had switched to Emacs sooner so that they would have gotten their hands on Magit earlier.

While one has to know the basic features of Emacs to be able to make full use of Magit, acquiring just enough Emacs skills doesn't take long and is worth it, even for users who prefer other editors. Vim users are advised to give Evil, the "Extensible VI Layer for Emacs", and Spacemacs, an "Emacs starter-kit focused on Evil" a try.

Magit provides a consistent and efficient Git porcelain. After a short learning period, you will be able to perform most of your daily version control tasks faster than you would on the command line. You will likely also start using features that seemed too daunting in the past.

Magit fully embraces Git. It exposes many advanced features using a simple but flexible interface instead of only wrapping the trivial ones like many GUI clients do. Of course Magit supports logging, cloning, pushing, and other commands that usually don't fail in spectacular ways; but it also supports tasks that often cannot be completed in a single step. Magit fully supports tasks such as merging, rebasing, cherry-picking, reverting, and blaming by not only providing a command to initiate these tasks but also by displaying context sensitive information along the way and providing commands that are useful for resolving conflicts and resuming the sequence after doing so.

Magit wraps and in many cases improves upon at least the following Git porcelain commands: `add`, `am`, `bisect`, `blame`, `branch`, `checkout`, `cherry`, `cherry-pick`, `clean`, `clone`, `commit`, `config`, `describe`, `diff`, `fetch`, `format-patch`, `init`, `log`, `merge`, `merge-tree`, `mv`, `notes`, `pull`, `rebase`, `reflog`, `remote`, `request-pull`, `reset`, `revert`, `rm`, `show`, `stash`, `submodule`, and `tag`. Many more Magit porcelain commands are implemented on top of Git plumbing commands.

2 Installation

Magit can be installed using Emacs' package manager or manually from its development repository.

2.1 Updating from an older release

When updating from `1.2.*` or `1.4.*`, you should first uninstall Magit and some of its dependencies and restart Emacs before installing the latest release.

- The old Magit installation has to be removed because some macros have changed and using the old definitions when building the new release would lead to very strange results, including compile errors. This is due to a limitation in Emacs' package manager or rather Emacs itself: it's not possible to reliably unload a feature or even all features belonging to a package.

- Furthermore the old dependencies `git-commit-mode` and `git-rebase-mode` have to be removed because they are no longer used by the `2.1.0` release and get in the way of their successors `git-commit` and `git-rebase`.

So please uninstall the packages `magit`, `git-commit-mode`, and `git-rebase-mode`. Then quit Emacs and start a new instance. Only then follow the instructions in either one of the next two sections.

Also note that starting with the `2.1.0` release, Magit requires at least Emacs `24.4` and Git `1.9.4`. You should make sure you have at least these releases installed before updating Magit. And if you connect to remote hosts using Tramp, then you should also make sure to install a recent enough Git version on these hosts.

2.2 Installing from an Elpa archive

If you are updating from a release older than `2.1.0`, then you have to first uninstall the old version. See Section 2.1 [Updating from an older release], page 3.

Magit is available from all three of the popular unofficial Elpa archives: Melpa, Melpa-Stable, and Marmalade. If you haven't used Emacs' package manager before, then it is high time you familiarize yourself with it by reading the documentation in the Emacs manual, see Section "Packages" in emacs. Then add one of the archives to `package-archives`:

- To use Melpa:

```
(require 'package)
(add-to-list 'package-archives
             '("melpa" . "http://melpa.org/packages/") t)
```

- To use Melpa-Stable:

```
(require 'package)
(add-to-list 'package-archives
             '("melpa-stable" . "http://stable.melpa.org/packages/") t)
```

- To use Marmalade:

```
(require 'package)
(add-to-list 'package-archives
             '("marmalade" . "http://marmalade-repo.org/packages/") t)
```

Once you have added your preferred archive, you need to update the local package list using:

```
M-x package-refresh-contents RET
```

Once you have done that, you can install Magit and its dependencies using:

```
M-x package-install RET magit RET
```

Now see Section 2.4 [Post-installation tasks], page 5.

2.3 Installing from the Git repository

If you are updating from a release older than 2.1.0, then you have to first uninstall the old version. See Section 2.1 [Updating from an older release], page 3.

Magit depends on the **dash** library, available from all three of the popular third-party Elpa archives. Install it using M-x install-package RET dash RET. Of course you may also install it manually from its development repository, but I won't cover that here.

Then clone the Magit repository:

```
$ git clone git://github.com/magit/magit.git ~/.emacs.d/site-lisp/magit
$ cd ~/.emacs.d/site-lisp/magit
```

Then compile the libraries and generate the info manuals:

```
$ make
```

If you haven't installed **dash** using Elpa or at */path/to/magit/../dash*, then you have to tell **make** where to find it. To do so create */path/to/magit/config.mk* with the following content before running **make**:

```
LOAD_PATH = -L /path/to/magit/lisp -L /path/to/dash
```

Finally add this to your init file:

```
(add-to-list 'load-path "~/.emacs.d/site-lisp/magit/lisp")
(require 'magit)

(with-eval-after-load 'info
  (info-initialize)
  (add-to-list 'Info-directory-list
               "~/.emacs.d/site-lisp/magit/Documentation/"))
```

Note that you have to add the **lisp/** subdirectory to the **load-path**, not the top-level of the repository.

Instead of requiring the feature **magit**, you could only load the autoloads, by loading the file *magit-autoloads.el*.

Instead of running Magit directly from the repository by adding that to the **load-path**, you might want to instead install it in some other directory using **sudo make install** and setting **load-path** accordingly.

To update Magit use:

```
$ git pull
$ make
```

At times it might be necessary to run **make clean all** instead.

To view all available targets use **make help**.

Now see Section 2.4 [Post-installation tasks], page 5.

2.4 Post-installation tasks

After installing Magit you should verify that you are indeed using the Magit, Git, and Emacs releases you think you are using. It's best to restart Emacs before doing so, to make sure you are not using an outdated value for `load-path`.

     `M-x magit-version RET`

should display something like

     `Magit 2.1.0, Git 2.4.2, Emacs 24.5.1`

Then you might also want to read about options that many users likely want to customize. See Section 9.2 [Essential settings], page 55.

To be able to follow cross references to Git manpages found in this manual, you might also have to manually install the `gitman` info manual, or advice **Info-follow-nearest-node** to instead open the actual manpage. See Section A.6 [How to install the gitman info manual?], page 70.

If you are completely new to Magit then see Chapter 3 [Getting started], page 6.

If you have used an older Magit release before, then you should have a look at the release notes `https://raw.githubusercontent.com/magit/magit/master/Documentation/RelNotes/2.1.0.txt`.

And last but not least please consider making a donation, to ensure that I can keep working on Magit. See `http://magit.vc/donations.html` for various donation options.

3 Getting started

This section describes the most essential features that many Magitians use on a daily basis. It only scratches the surface but should be enough to get you started.

(You might want to create a repository just for this walk-through, e.g. by cloning an existing repository. If you don't use a separate repository then make sure you create a snapshot as described below).

To display information about the current Git repository, type M-x magit-status. You will be doing that so often that it is best to bind this command globally:

    (global-set-key (kbd "C-x g") 'magit-status)

Most Magit commands are commonly invoked from this buffer. It should be considered the primary interface to interact with Git using Magit. There are many other Magit buffers, but they are usually created from this buffer.

Depending on what state your repository is in, this buffer will contain sections titled "Staged changes", "Unstaged changes", "Unpulled commits", "Unpushed commits", and/or some others.

If some staged and/or unstaged changes exist, you should back them up now. Type z to show the stashing popup buffer featuring various stash variants and arguments that can be passed to these commands. Do not worry about those for now, just type Z (uppercase) to create a stash while also keeping the index and work tree intact. The status buffer should now also contain a section titled "Stashes".

Otherwise, if there are no uncommitted changes, you should create some now by editing and saving some of the tracked files. Then go back to the status buffer, while at the same time refreshing it, by typing C-x g. (When the status buffer, or any Magit buffer for that matter, is the current buffer, then you can also use just g to refresh it).

Move between sections using p and n. Note that the bodies of some sections are hidden. Type TAB to expand or collapse the section at point. You can also use C-tab to cycle the visibility of the current section and its children. Move to a file section inside the section named "Unstaged changes" and type s to stage the changes you have made to that file. That file now appears under "Staged changes".

Magit can stage and unstage individual hunks, not just complete files. Move to the file you have just staged, expand it using TAB, move to one of the hunks using n, and unstage just that by typing u. Note how the staging (s) and unstaging (u) commands operate on the change at point. Many other commands behave the same way.

You can also un-/stage just part of a hunk. Inside the body of a hunk section (move there using C-n), set the mark using C-SPC and move down until some added and removed lines fall inside the region but not all of them. Again type s to stage.

It's also possible to un-/stage multiple files at once. Move to a file section, type C-SPC, move to the next file using n, and then s to stage both files. Note that both the mark and point have to be on the headings of sibling sections for this to work. If the region looks like it does in other buffers, then it doesn't select Magit sections that can be acted on as a unit.

And then of course you want to commit your changes. Type c. This shows the commit-ting popup buffer featuring various commit variants and arguments that can be passed to `git commit`. Do not worry about those for now. We want to create a "normal" commit, which is done by typing `c` again.

Now two new buffers appear. One is for writing the commit message, the other shows a diff with the changes that are about to committed. Write a message and then type `C-c` `C-c` to actually create the commit.

You probably don't want to push the commit you just created because you just committed some random changes, but if that is not the case you could push it by typing `P` to bring up the push popup and then `P` again to push to the configured upstream. (If the upstream is not configured, then you would be prompted for the push target instead.)

Instead we are going to undo the changes made so far. Bring up the log for the current branch by typing `l l`, move to the last commit created before starting with this walk through using `n`, and do a hard reset using `C-u x`. **WARNING**: this discards all uncommitted changes. If you did not follow the advice about using a separate repository for these experiments and did not create a snapshot of uncommitted changes before starting to try out Magit, then don't do this.

So far we have mentioned the commit, push, and log popups. These are probably among the popups you will be using the most, but many others exist. To show a popup with all other popups (and some other commands which are not popups), type `h`. Try a few.

In most cases the key bindings in that popup correspond to the bindings in Magit buffers, including but not limited to the status buffer. So you could type `h d` to bring up the diff popup, but once you remember that "d" stands for "diff", you would usually do so by just typing `d`. But the "popup of popups" is useful even once you have memorized all the bindings, as it can provide easy access to Magit commands from non-Magit buffers. So you should bind this globally too:

```
(global-set-key (kbd "C-x M-g") 'magit-dispatch-popup)
```

4 Interface concepts

4.1 Modes and Buffers

Magit provides several major modes. For each of these modes there usually exists only one buffer per repository. Separate modes and thus buffers exist for commits, diffs, logs, and some other things.

In this manual we often speak about "Magit buffers". By that we mean buffers whose major-modes derive from `magit-mode`.

Besides these special purpose buffers, there also exists an overview buffer, called the **status buffer**. Its usually from this buffer that the user invokes Git commands, or creates or visits other buffers.

q   (`magit-mode-bury-buffer`)

> This command buries the current Magit buffer. With a prefix argument, it instead kills the buffer.
>
> If `magit-restore-window-configuration` is non-nil and the last configuration stored by `magit-mode-display-buffer` originates from the selected frame (which usually is the case), then that is restored after burying or killing the buffer.

`magit-restore-window-configuration`   [User Option]

> This option controls whether quitting a Magit buffer restores the previous window configuration.

While it often is enough to have one buffer of a certain Magit mode per repository, this is not always the case. You might, for example, want to view the diffs for two commits at the same time. To do so, first rename the existing revision buffer. Then show another commit. Usually that would reuse the existing buffer, but because its name no longer matches the default name, a new buffer is created instead. The new buffer uses the default name, and therefore will be reused to show other commits as usual.

M-x magit-rename-buffer   (`magit-rename-buffer`)

> This command changes the name of the current Magit buffer by appending `<N>` and thereby keeping Magit from re-using it to display other information of the same kind.
>
> With a prefix argument, the user can pick an arbitrary name.

4.2 Automatic save

File-visiting buffers are by default saved at certain points in time. This doesn't guarantee that Magit buffers are always up-to-date, but, provided one only edits files by editing them in Emacs and uses only Magit to interact with Git, one can be fairly confident. When in doubt or after outside changes, type **g** (`magit-refresh`) to save and refresh explicitly.

`magit-save-repository-buffers`   [User Option]

> This option controls whether file-visiting buffers are saved before certain events.

If this is non-nil then all modified file-visiting buffers belonging to the current repository may be saved before running commands, before creating new Magit buffers, and before explicitly refreshing such buffers. If this is `dontask` then this is done without user intervention. If it is `t` then the user has to confirm each save.

4.3 Automatic refresh and revert

After running a command which may change the state of the current repository, the current Magit buffer and the corresponding status buffer are refreshed. This ensures that the displayed information is up-to-date but can lead to a noticeable delay in big repositories. Other Magit buffers are not refreshed to keep the delay to a minimum and also because doing so can sometimes be undesirable.

`magit-revert-buffers`   [User Option]

    This option controls if and how file-visiting buffers in the current repository are reverted.

    Unmodified buffers visiting files belonging to the current repository may be reverted after refreshing the current Magit buffer and after running certain other commands.

- `nil`

  Don't revert any buffers.

- `ask`

  List the buffers which might potentially have to be reverted and ask the user whether she wants to revert them. If so, then do it synchronously.

- `t`

  Revert the buffers synchronously, mentioning each one as it is being reverted and then also show a summary in the echo area.

- `usage`

  Like `t` but include usage information in the summary. This is the default so that users come here and pick what is right for them.

- `silent`

  Revert the buffers synchronously and be quiet about it.

- NUMBER

  An integer or float. Revert the buffers asynchronously, mentioning each one as it is being reverted. If user input arrives, then stop reverting. After NUMBER seconds resume reverting.

Buffers can also be refreshed explicitly, which is useful in buffers that weren't current during the last refresh and after changes were made to the repository outside of Magit.

`g` (`magit-refresh`)

    This command refreshes the current buffer if its major mode derives from `magit-mode` as well as the corresponding status buffer.

    If the option `magit-revert-buffers` calls for it, then it also reverts all unmodified buffers that visit files being tracked in the current repository.

G   (`magit-refresh-all`)

> This command refreshes all Magit buffers belonging to the current repository and also reverts all unmodified buffers that visit files being tracked in the current repository.
>
> The file-visiting buffers are always reverted, even if `magit-revert-buffers` is nil.

`magit-refresh-buffer-hook`   [User Option]

> This hook is run in each Magit buffer that was refreshed during the current refresh - normally the current buffer and the status buffer.

`magit-after-revert-hook`   [User Option]

> This hook is run in each file-visiting buffer belonging to the current repository that was actually reverted during a refresh.
>
> Note that adding something here is very expensive. If you experience performance issues, you might want to check this hook, as well as `magit-not-reverted-hook` and, if possible, remove some of the functions added by third-party packages.

`magit-not-reverted-hook`   [User Option]

> This hook is run in each file-visiting buffer belonging to the current repository that was reverted during a refresh. The file was not reverted because it did not change, and so Magit does not have to do anything. This hook is intended for third-party extensions that need to run some functions even on such files.

4.4 Sections

Magit buffers are organized into nested sections, which can be collapsed and expanded, similar to how sections are handled in Org mode. Each section also has a type, and some sections also have a value. For each section type there can also be a local keymap, shared by all sections of that type.

Taking advantage the section value and type, many commands operate on the current section, or when the region is active and selects sections of the same type, all of the selected sections. Commands that only make sense for a particular section type (as opposed to just behaving differently depending on the type) are usually bound in section type keymaps.

4.4.1 Section movement

To move within a section use the usual keys (`C-p`, `C-n`, `C-b`, `C-f` etc), whose global bindings are not shadowed. To move to another section use the following commands.

p   (`magit-section-backward`)

> When not at the beginning of a section, then move to the beginning of the current section. At the beginning of a section, instead move to the beginning of the previous visible section.

n   (`magit-section-forward`)

> Move to the beginning of the next visible section.

P   (`magit-section-backward-siblings`)

> Move to the beginning of the previous sibling section. If there is no previous sibling section, then move to the parent section instead.

N   (magit-section-forward-siblings)
> Move to the beginning of the next sibling section. If there is no next sibling section, then move to the parent section instead.

^   (magit-section-up)
> Move to the beginning of the parent of the current section.

The above commands all call the hook `magit-section-movement-hook`. And, except for the second, the below functions are all members of that hook's default value.

`magit-section-movement-hook`   [Variable]
> This hook is run by all of the above movement commands, after arriving at the destination.

`magit-hunk-set-window-start`   [Function]
> This hook function ensures that the beginning of the current section is visible, provided it is a `hunk` section. Otherwise, it does nothing.

`magit-section-set-window-start`   [Function]
> This hook function ensures that the beginning of the current section is visible, regardless of the section's type. If you add this to `magit-section-movement-hook`, then you must remove the hunk-only variant in turn.

`magit-log-maybe-show-commit`   [Function]
> This hook function shows the commit at point in another window. If the section at point is a `commit` section and the value of `magit-diff-auto-show-p` calls for it, then the commit is shown in another window, using `magit-show-commit`.

`magit-log-maybe-show-more-commits`   [Function]
> This hook function only has an effect in log buffers, and `point` is on the "show more" section. If that is the case, then it doubles the number of commits that are being shown.

4.4.2 Section visibility

Magit provides many commands for changing the visibility of sections, but all you need to get started are the next two.

TAB   (magit-section-toggle)
> Toggle the visibility of the body of the current section.

C-<tab>   (magit-section-cycle)
> Cycle the visibility of current section and its children.

M-<tab>   (magit-section-cycle-diffs)
> Cycle the visibility of diff-related sections in the current buffer.

s-<tab>   (magit-section-cycle-global)
> Cycle the visibility of all sections in the current buffer.

`magit-section-show-level-1`   [Command]
`magit-section-show-level-2`   [Command]
`magit-section-show-level-3`   [Command]

`magit-section-show-level-4`   [Command]
>   To show sections surrounding the current section, up to level N, press the respective
>   number key (1, 2, 3, or 4).

`magit-section-show-level-1-all`   [Command]
`magit-section-show-level-2-all`   [Command]
`magit-section-show-level-3-all`   [Command]
`magit-section-show-level-4-all`   [Command]
>   To show all sections up to level N, press the respective number key and meta (M-1,
>   M-2, M-3, or M-4).

Some functions, which are used to implement the above commands, are also exposed
as commands themselves. By default no keys are bound to these commands, as they are
generally perceived to be much less useful. But your mileage may vary.

`magit-section-show`   [Command]
>   Show the body of the current section.

`magit-section-hide`   [Command]
>   Hide the body of the current section.

`magit-section-show-headings`   [Command]
>   Recursively show headings of children of the current section. Only show the headings.
>   Previously shown text-only bodies are hidden.

`magit-section-show-children`   [Command]
>   Recursively show the bodies of children of the current section. With a prefix argument
>   show children down to the level of the currect section, and hide deeper children.

`magit-section-hide-children`   [Command]
>   Recursively hide the bodies of children of the current section.

`magit-section-toggle-children`   [Command]
>   Toggle visibility of bodies of children of the current section.

When a buffer is first created then some sections are shown expanded while others
are not. This is hard coded. When a buffer is refreshed then the previous visibility is
preserved. The initial visibility of certain sections can also be overwritten using the hook
`magit-section-set-visibility-hook`.

`magit-section-set-visibility-hook`   [Variable]
>   This hook is run when first creating a buffer and also when refreshing an existing
>   buffer, and is used to determine the visibility of the section currently being inserted.
>
>   Each function is called with one argument, the section being inserted. It should return
>   `hide` or `show`, or to leave the visibility undefined `nil`. If no function decides on the
>   visibility and the buffer is being refreshed, then the visibility is preserved; or if the
>   buffer is being created, then the hard coded default is used.
>
>   Usually this should only be used to set the initial visibility but not during refreshes.
>   If `magit-insert-section--oldroot` is non-nil, then the buffer is being refreshed and
>   these functions should immediately return `nil`.

4.4.3 Section hooks

Which sections are inserted into certain buffers is controlled with hooks. This includes the status and the refs buffers. For other buffers, e.g. log, diff, and revision buffers, this is not possible.

For buffers whose sections can be customized by the user, a hook variable called `magit-TYPE-sections-hook` exists. This hook should be changed using `magit-add-section-hook`. Avoid using `add-hooks` or the Custom interface.

The various available section hook variables are described later in this manual along with the appropriate "section inserter functions".

`magit-add-section-hook` *hook function* **&optional** *at append local*   [Function]
> Add the function FUNCTION to the value of section hook HOOK.
>
> Add FUNCTION at the beginning of the hook list unless optional APPEND is non-nil, in which case FUNCTION is added at the end. If FUNCTION already is a member then move it to the new location.
>
> If optional AT is non-nil and a member of the hook list, then add FUNCTION next to that instead. Add before or after AT depending on APPEND. If only FUNCTION is a member of the list, then leave it wherever it already is.
>
> If optional LOCAL is non-nil, then modify the hook's buffer-local value rather than its global value. This makes the hook local by copying the default value. That copy is then modified.
>
> HOOK should be a symbol. If HOOK is void, it is first set to nil. HOOK's value must not be a single hook function. FUNCTION should be a function that takes no arguments and inserts one or multiple sections at point, moving point forward. FUNCTION may choose not to insert its section(s), when doing so would not make sense. It should not be abused for other side-effects.

To remove a function from a section hook, use `remove-hook`.

4.4.4 Section types and values

Each section has a type, for example `hunk`, `file`, and `commit`. Instances of certain section types also have a value. The value of a section of type `file`, for example, is a file name.

Users usually do not have to worry about a section's type and value, but knowing them can be handy at times.

M-x magit-describe-section   (magit-describe-section)
> Show information about the section at point in the echo area, as "VALUE [TYPE PARENT-TYPE...] BEGINNING-END".

Many commands behave differently depending on the type of the section at point and/or somehow consume the value of that section. But that is only one of the reasons why the same key may do something different, depending on what section is current.

Additionally for each section type a keymap **might** be defined, named `magit-TYPE-section-map`. That keymap is used as text property keymap of all text belonging to any section of the respective type. If such a map does not exist for a certain type, then you can define it yourself, and it will automatically be used.

4.4.5 Section options

This section describes options that have an effect on more than just a certain type of sections. As you can see there are not many of those.

`magit-section-show-child-count`   [User Option]
> Whether to append the number of children to section headings. This only affects sections that could benefit from this information.

4.5 Popup buffers and prefix commands

Many Magit commands are implemented using **popup buffers**. First the user invokes a **popup** or **prefix** command, which causes a popup buffer with the available **infix** arguments and **suffix** commands to be displayed. The user then optionally toggles/sets some arguments and finally invokes one of the suffix commands.

This is implemented in the library `magit-popup`. Earlier releases used the library `magit-key-mode`. A future release will switch to a yet-to-be-written successor, which will likely be named `transient`.

Because `magit-popup` can also be used by other packages without having to depend on all of Magit, it is documented in its own manual. See `magit-popup`.

`C-c C-c`   (`magit-dispatch-popup`)
> This popup command shows a buffer featuring all other Magit popup commands as well as some other commands that are not popup commands themselves.

This command is also, or especially, useful outside Magit buffers, so you should setup a global binding:

```
(global-set-key (kbd "C-x M-g") 'magit-dispatch-popup)
```

4.6 Completion and confirmation

Many commands read a value from the user. By default this is done using the built-in function `completing-read`, but Magit can instead use another completion framework.

`magit-completing-read-function`   [User Option]
> The value of this variable is the function used to perform completion. Because functions *intended* to replace `completing-read` often are not fully compatible drop-in replacements, and also because Magit expects them to add the default choice to the prompt themselves, such functions should not be used directly. Instead a wrapper function has to be used.

> Currently only the real `completing-read` and Ido are fully supported. More frameworks will be supported in the future.

`magit-builtin-completing-read` *prompt choices* **&optional** *predicate*   [Function]
> *require-match initial-input hist def*
> Perform completion using `completion-read`.

`magit-ido-completing-read` *prompt choices* **&optional** *predicate*   [Function]
        require-match initial-input hist def
    Perform completion using `ido-completing-read+` from the package by the same
    name (which you have to explicitly install). Ido itself comes with a supposed drop-
    in replacement `ido-completing-read`, but that has too many deficits to serve our
    needs.

By default many commands that could potentially lead to data loss have to be confirmed.
This includes many very common commands, so this can become annoying quickly. Many
of these actions can be undone, provided `magit-wip-before-change-mode` is turned on
(which it is not by default, due to performance concerns).

`magit-no-confirm`   [User Option]
    The value of this option is a list of symbols, representing commands which do not
    have to be confirmed by the user before being carried out.

    When the global mode `magit-wip-before-change-mode` is enabled then many com-
    mands can be undone. If that mode is enabled then adding `safe-with-wip` to
    this list has the same effect as adding `discard`, `reverse`, `stage-all-changes`, and
    `unstage-all-changes`.

```
(add-to-list 'magit-no-confirm 'safe-with-wip)
```

    For a list of all symbols that can be added to the value of this variable, see the
    doc-string.

Note that there are commands that ignore this option and always require confirmation,
or which can be told not to do so using another dedicated option. Also most commands,
when acting on multiple sections at once always, require confirmation, even when they do
respect this option when acting on a single section.

4.7 Running Git

4.7.1 Viewing Git output

Magit runs Git either for side-effects (e.g. when pushing) or to get some value (e.g. the
name of the current branch). When Git is run for side-effects then the output goes into a
per-repository log buffer, which can be consulted when things don't go as expected.

$ (`magit-process`)
    This commands displays the process buffer for the current repository.

Inside that buffer, the usual key bindings for navigating and showing sections are available. There is one additional command.

k   (`magit-process-kill`)
    This command kills the process represented by the section at point.

`magit-git-debug`   [User Option]
    When this is non-nil then the output of all calls to git are logged in the process buffer.
    This is useful when debugging, otherwise it just negatively affects performance.

4.7.2 Running Git manually

While Magit provides many Emacs commands to interact with Git, it does not cover everything. In those cases your existing Git knowledge will come in handy. Magit provides some commands for running arbitrary Git commands by typing them into the minibuffer, instead of having to switch to a shell.

!   (`magit-run-popup`)

        Show the popup buffer featuring the below suffix commands.

! !   (`magit-git-command-topdir`)

        Execute a Git subcommand asynchronously, displaying the output.

        With a prefix argument run Git in the root of the current repository.

! :   (`magit-git-command`)

        Execute a Git subcommand asynchronously, displaying the output. Run Git in the top-level directory of the current repository.

  This popup also features some commands that start external gui tools.

! g (`magit-run-git-gui`)

        Run `git gui` for the current git repository.

! k (`magit-run-gitk`)

        Run Gitk for the current git repository.

        Run `gitk --all`. With a prefix argument run gitk without any arguments.

4.7.3 Git executable

Except on MS Windows, Magit defaults to running Git without specifying the path to the git executable. Instead the first executable found by Emacs on `exec-path` is used (whose value in turn is set based on the value of the environment variable `$PATH` when Emacs was started).

This has the advantage that it continues to work even when using Tramp to connect to a remote machine on which the executable is found in a different place. The downside is that if you have multiple versions of Git installed, then you might end up using another version than the one you think you are using.

M-x magit-version   (`magit-version`)

        Shows the currently used versions of Magit, Git, and Emacs in the echo area. Non-interactively this just returns the Magit version.

When the `system-type` is `windows-nt`, then `magit-git-executable` is set to an absolute path when Magit is first loaded. This is necessary because Git on that platform comes with several wrapper scripts for the actual git binary, which are also placed on `$PATH`, and using one of these wrappers instead of the binary would degrade performance horribly.

If Magit doesn't find the correct executable then you **can** work around that by setting `magit-git-executable` to an absolute path. But note that doing so is a kludge. It is better to make sure the order in the environment variable `$PATH` is correct, and that Emacs is started with that environment in effect. If you have to connect from Windows to a non-Windows machine, then you must change the value to "git".

`magit-git-executable`   [User Option]

  The git executable used by Magit, either the full path to the executable or the string
  "git" to let Emacs find the executable itself, using the standard mechanism for doing
  such things.

4.7.4 Global Git arguments

`magit-git-global-arguments`   [User Option]

  The arguments set here are used every time the git executable is run as a subprocess.
  They are placed right after the executable itself and before the git command - as in
  `git HERE... COMMAND REST`. For valid arguments see the git(1) manpage .

  Be careful what you add here, especially if you are using Tramp to connect to servers
  with ancient Git versions. Never remove anything that is part of the default value,
  unless you really know what you are doing. And think very hard before adding
  something; it will be used every time Magit runs Git for any purpose.

5 Inspecting

The functionality provided by Magit can be roughly divided into three groups: inspecting existing data, manipulating existing data or adding new data, and transferring data. Of course that is a rather crude distinction that often falls short, but it's more useful than no distinction at all. This section is concerned with inspecting data, the next two with manipulating and transferring it. Then follows a section about miscellaneous functionality, which cannot easily be fit into this distinction.

Of course other distinctions make sense too, e.g. Git's distinction between porcelain and plumbing commands, which for the most part is equivalent to Emacs' distinction between interactive commands and non-interactive functions. All of the sections mentioned before are mainly concerned with the porcelain – Magit's plumbing layer is described later.

5.1 Status buffer

While other Magit buffers contain e.g. one particular diff or one particular log, the status buffer contains the diffs for staged and unstaged changes, logs for unpushed and unpulled commits, lists of stashes and untracked files, and information related to the current branch.

During certain incomplete operations – for example when a merge resulted in a conflict – additional information is displayed that helps proceeding with or aborting the operation.

The command `magit-status` displays the status buffer belonging to the current repository in another window. This command is used so often that it should be bound globally. We recommend using `C-x g`:

```
(global-set-key (kbd "C-x g") 'magit-status)
```

C-x g   (`magit-status`)

> Show the status of the current Git repository in a buffer. With a prefix argument prompt for a repository to be shown. With two prefix arguments prompt for an arbitrary directory. If that directory isn't the root of an existing repository, then offer to initialize it as a new repository.

`magit-repository-directories`   [User Option]

> Directories containing Git repositories. Magit checks these directories for Git repositories and offers them as choices when `magit-status` is used with a prefix argument.

`magit-repository-directories-depth`   [User Option]

> The maximum depth to look for Git repositories. When looking for a Git repository below the directories in `magit-repository-directories`, only descend this many levels deep.

`ido-enter-magit-status`   [Command]

> From an Ido prompt used to open a file, instead drop into `magit-status`. This is similar to `ido-magic-delete-char`, which, despite its name, usually causes a Dired buffer to be created.

> To make this command available, use something like:

```
(add-hook 'ido-setup-hook
          (lambda ()
```

```
(define-key ido-completion-map
  (kbd \"C-x g\") 'ido-enter-magit-status)))
```

Starting with Emacs 25.1 that keymap can also be customized in a sane fashion:

```
(define-key ido-completion-map
  (kbd \"C-x g\") 'ido-enter-magit-status)))
```

5.1.1 Status sections

The contents of status buffers is controlled using the hook `magit-status-sections-hook`. See Section 4.4.3 [Section hooks], page 13 to learn about such hooks and how to customize them.

`magit-status-sections-hook`   [User Option]

> Hook run to insert sections into a status buffer.

The first function on that hook by default is `magit-insert-status-headers`; it is described in the next section. By default the following functions are also members of that hook:

`magit-insert-merge-log`   [Function]

> Insert section for the on-going merge. Display the heads that are being merged. If no merge is in progress, do nothing.

`magit-insert-rebase-sequence`   [Function]

> Insert section for the on-going rebase sequence. If no such sequence is in progress, do nothing.

`magit-insert-am-sequence`   [Function]

> Insert section for the on-going patch applying sequence. If no such sequence is in progress, do nothing.

`magit-insert-sequencer-sequence`   [Function]

> Insert section for the on-going cherry-pick or revert sequence. If no such sequence is in progress, do nothing.

`magit-insert-bisect-output`   [Function]

> While bisecting, insert section with output from `git bisect`.

`magit-insert-bisect-rest`   [Function]

> While bisecting, insert section visualizing the bisect state.

`magit-insert-bisect-log`   [Function]

> While bisecting, insert section logging bisect progress.

`magit-insert-untracked-files`   [Function]

> Maybe insert a list or tree of untracked files. Do so depending on the value of `status.showUntrackedFiles`.

`magit-insert-unstaged-changes`   [Function]

> Insert section showing unstaged changes.

`magit-insert-staged-changes`   [Function]
  Insert section showing staged changes.

`magit-insert-stashes` **&optional** *ref heading*   [Function]
  Insert the `stashes` section showing reflog for "refs/stash". If optional REF is non-nil
  show reflog for that instead. If optional HEADING is non-nil use that as section
  heading instead of "Stashes:".

`magit-insert-unpulled-commits`   [Function]
  Insert section showing unpulled commits.

`magit-insert-unpushed-commits`   [Function]
  Insert section showing unpushed commits.

  The following functions can also be added to the above hook:

`magit-insert-tracked-files`   [Function]
  Insert a tree of tracked files.

`magit-insert-unpulled-or-recent-commits`   [Function]
  Insert section showing unpulled or recent commits. If an upstream is configured for
  the current branch and it is ahead of the current branch, then show the missing
  commits. Otherwise, show the last `magit-log-section-commit-count` commits.

`magit-insert-recent-commits`   [Function]
  Insert section showing the last `magit-log-section-commit-count` commits.

`magit-log-section-commit-count`   [User Option]
  How many recent commits `magit-insert-recent-commits` and `magit-insert-`
  `unpulled-or-recent-commits` (provided there are no unpulled commits)
  show.

`magit-insert-unpulled-cherries`   [Function]
  Insert section showing unpulled commits. Like `magit-insert-unpulled-commits`
  but prefix each commit that has not been applied yet (i.e. a commit with a patch-id
  not shared with any local commit) with "+", and all others with "-".

`magit-insert-unpulled-module-commits`   [Function]
  Insert sections for all submodules with unpulled commits. These sections can be
  expanded to show the respective commits.

`magit-insert-unpushed-cherries`   [Function]
  Insert section showing unpushed commits. Like `magit-insert-unpushed-commits`
  but prefix each commit which has not been applied to upstream yet (i.e. a commit
  with a patch-id not shared with any upstream commit) with "+" and all others with
  "-".

`magit-insert-unpushed-module-commits`   [Function]
  Insert sections for all submodules with unpushed commits. These sections can be
  expanded to show the respective commits.

  See Section 5.5 [References buffer], page 28 for some more section inserters, which could
be used here.

5.1.2 Status header sections

The contents of status buffers is controlled using the hook `magit-status-sections-hook`, as described in the previous section. By default `magit-insert-status-headers` is the first member of that hook variable.

`magit-insert-status-headers`   [Function]

Insert headers sections appropriate for `magit-status-mode` buffers. The sections are inserted by running the functions on the hook `magit-status-headers-hook`.

`magit-status-headers-hook`   [User Option]

Hook run to insert headers sections into the status buffer.

This hook is run by `magit-insert-status-headers`, which in turn has to be a member of `magit-insert-status-sections` to be used at all.

By default the following functions are members of the above hook:

`magit-insert-head-header`   [Function]

Insert a header line about the `HEAD` commit.

`magit-insert-upstream-header`   [Function]

Insert a header line about the upstream branch and its tip.

`magit-insert-tags-header`   [Function]

Insert a header line about the current and/or next tag.

The following functions can also be added to the above hook:

`magit-insert-repo-header`   [Function]

Insert a header line showing the path to the repository top-level.

`magit-insert-remote-header`   [Function]

Insert a header line about the remote of the current branch.

5.1.3 Status options

`magit-status-refresh-hook`   [User Option]

Hook run after a status buffer has been refreshed.

`magit-status-buffer-switch-function`   [User Option]

Function used by `magit-status` to switch to a status buffer. The function is given one argument, the status buffer.

`magit-status-buffer-name-format`   [User Option]

Name format for buffers used to display a repository's status.

The following `format`-like specs are supported: `%a` the absolute filename of the repository top-level. `%b` the basename of the repository top-level.

`magit-log-section-args`   [User Option]

Additional Git arguments used when creating log sections. Only `--graph`, `--decorate`, and `--show-signature` are supported. This option is only a temporary kludge and will be removed.

Note that due to an issue in Git the use of `--graph` is very slow with long histories, so you probably don't want to add this here.

Also see the proceeding section for more options concerning status buffers.

5.2 Logging

Also see the git-log(1) manpage .

l   (magit-log-popup)
>   This prefix commands shows the following suffix commands along with the
>   appropriate infix arguments in a popup buffer.

l l   (magit-log-current)
>   Show log for the current branch. When HEAD is detached or with a prefix
>   argument, show log for one or more revs read from the minibuffer.

l o   (magit-log)
>   Show log for one or more revs read from the minibuffer. The user can input any
>   revision or revisions separated by a space, or even ranges, but only branches,
>   tags, and a representation of the commit at point are available as completion
>   candidates.

l h   (magit-log-head)
>   Show log for HEAD.

l L   (magit-log-branches)
>   Show log for all local branches and HEAD.

l b   (magit-log-all-branches)
>   Show log for all local and remote branches and HEAD.

l a   (magit-log-all)
>   Show log for all references and HEAD.

The following related commands are not available from the popup.

Y   (magit-cherry)
>   Show commits in a branch that are not merged in the upstream branch.

M-x magit-log-buffer-file   (magit-log-buffer-file)
>   Show log for the file visited in the current buffer.

5.2.1 Log Buffer

C-c C-b   (magit-go-backward)
>   Move backward in current buffer's history.

C-c C-f   (magit-go-forward)
>   Move forward in current buffer's history.

SPC   (magit-diff-show-or-scroll-up)
>   Update the commit or diff buffer for the thing at point.

>   Either show the commit or stash at point in the appropriate buffer, or if that
>   buffer is already being displayed in the current frame and contains information
>   about that commit or stash, then instead scroll the buffer up. If there is no
>   commit or stash at point, then prompt for a commit.

DEL   (`magit-diff-show-or-scroll-down`)

> Update the commit or diff buffer for the thing at point.
>
> Either show the commit or stash at point in the appropriate buffer, or if that buffer is already being displayed in the current frame and contains information about that commit or stash, then instead scroll the buffer down. If there is no commit or stash at point, then prompt for a commit.

q   (`magit-log-bury-buffer`)

> Bury the current buffer or the revision buffer in the same frame. Like `magit-mode-bury-buffer` (which see) but with a negative prefix argument instead bury the revision buffer, provided it is displayed in the current frame.

`magit-log-auto-more`   [User Option]

> Insert more log entries automatically when moving past the last entry. Only considered when moving past the last entry with `magit-goto-*-section` commands.

+   (`magit-log-show-more-commits`)

> Increase the number of commits shown in current log.
>
> With no prefix argument, show twice as many commits as before. With a numerical prefix argument, show this many additional commits. With a non-numeric prefix argument, show all commits.
>
> When no limit was previously imposed in the current buffer, set the local limit to the default limit instead (or if that is nil then 100), regardless of the prefix argument.
>
> By default `magit-log-cutoff-length` commits are shown.

`magit-log-show-margin`   [User Option]

> Whether to initially show the margin in log buffers.
>
> When non-nil the author name and date are initially displayed in the margin of log buffers. The margin can be shown or hidden in the current buffer using the command `magit-toggle-margin`.
>
> When a log buffer contains a verbose log, then the margin is never displayed. In status buffers this option is ignored, but it is possible to show the margin using the mentioned command.

L   (`magit-toggle-margin`)

> Show or hide the Magit margin.

`magit-log-cutoff-length`   [User Option]

> The maximum number of commits to show in log and reflog buffers.

5.2.2 Select from log

When the user has to select a recent commit that is reachable from `HEAD`, using regular completion would be inconvenient (because most humans cannot remember hashes or "HEAD~5", at least not without double checking). Instead a log buffer is used to select the commit, which has the advantage that commits are presented in order and with the commit message. The following additional key bindings are available when a log is used for selection:

C-c C-c   (`magit-log-select-pick`)
> Select the commit at point and act on it. Call `magit-log-select-pick-function` with the selected commit as argument.

C-c C-k   (`magit-log-select-quit`)
> Abort selecting a commit, don't act on any commit.

This feature is used by rebase and squash commands.

5.2.3 Reflog

Also see the git-reflog(1) manpage .

These reflog commands are available from the log popup. See Section 5.2 [Logging], page 22.

l r   (`magit-reflog-current`)
> Display the reflog of the current branch.

l O   (`magit-reflog-other`)
> Display the reflog of a branch.

l H   (`magit-reflog-head`)
> Display the `HEAD` reflog.

5.3 Diffing

Also see the git-diff(1) manpage .

d   (`magit-diff-popup`)
> This prefix commands shows the following suffix commands along with the appropriate infix arguments in a popup buffer.

d d   (`magit-diff-dwim`)
> Show changes for the thing at point.

d r   (`magit-diff`)
> Show differences between two commits.
>
> RANGE should be a range (A..B or A...B) but can also be a single commit. If one side of the range is omitted, then it defaults to HEAD. If just a commit is given, then changes in the working tree relative to that commit are shown.

d w   (`magit-diff-worktree`)
> Show changes between the current working tree and the `HEAD` commit. With a prefix argument show changes between the working tree and a commit read from the minibuffer.

d s   (`magit-diff-staged`)
> Show changes between the index and the `HEAD` commit. With a prefix argument show changes between the index and a commit read from the minibuffer.

d u   (`magit-diff-unstaged`)
> Show changes between the working tree and the index.

d p   (`magit-diff-paths`)
> Show changes between any two files on disk.

d c   (`magit-show-commit`)
>   Show the commit at point. If there is no commit at point or with a prefix
>   argument, prompt for a commit.

d t   (`magit-stash-show`)
>   Show all diffs of a stash in a buffer.

M-x magit-diff-unpushed   (`magit-diff-unpushed`)
>   Show unpushed changes.

M-x magit-diff-unpulled   (`magit-diff-unpulled`)
>   Show unpulled changes.

5.3.1 Refreshing diffs

The `magit-diff-popup` described in the previous section is used to display a log in the
current repositories diff buffer. The following popup is used to change the arguments used
to generate the diff or diffs in the current buffer, the status buffer or the diff buffer.

In the diff buffer you can of course just use `magit-diff-popup`, but `magit-diff-refresh-popup` is more convenient because you don't have to again specify which differences
to show. In the status buffer this popup is the only way to change certain arguments.

D   (`magit-diff-refresh-popup`)
>   This prefix commands shows the following suffix commands along with the
>   appropriate infix arguments in a popup buffer.

D g   (`magit-diff-refresh`)
>   Set the local diff arguments for the current buffer.

D s   (`magit-diff-set-default-arguments`)
>   Set the global diff arguments for the current buffer.

D w   (`magit-diff-save-default-arguments`)
>   Set and save the global diff arguments for the current buffer.

D t   (`magit-diff-toggle-refine-hunk`)
>   Toggle hunk refinement on or off.

In addition to the above popup, which allow changing any of the supported arguments,
there also exist some commands which change a particular argument.

-   (`magit-diff-less-context`)
>   Decrease the context for diff hunks by COUNT lines.

+   (`magit-diff-more-context`)
>   Increase the context for diff hunks by COUNT lines.

0   (`magit-diff-default-context`)
>   Reset context for diff hunks to the default height.

While all of the above commands change **how** some change is being displayed without
changing **what** change is being displayed, the following commands do the opposite: they
change what is being displayed but not how.

C-c C-d   (`magit-diff-while-committing`)
> While committing, show the changes that are about to be committed. While amending, invoking the command again toggles between showing just the new changes or all the changes that will be committed.
>
> This binding is available in the diff buffer as well as the commit message buffer.

C-c C-b   (`magit-go-backward`)
> Move backward in current buffer's history.

C-c C-f   (`magit-go-forward`)
> Move forward in current buffer's history.

5.3.2 Diff buffer

RET   (`magit-diff-visit-file`)
> From a diff, visit the corresponding file at the appropriate position.
>
> When the file is already being displayed in another window of the same frame, then just select that window and adjust point. With a prefix argument also display in another window.
>
> If the diff shows changes in the worktree, the index, or **HEAD**, then visit the actual file. Otherwise when the diff is about an older commit, then visit the respective blob using `magit-find-file`. Also see `magit-diff-visit-file-worktree`, which, as the name suggests, always visits the actual file.

C-<return>   (`magit-diff-visit-file-worktree`)
> From a diff, visit the corresponding file at the appropriate position.
>
> When the file is already being displayed in another window of the same frame, then just select that window and adjust point. With a prefix argument also display in another window.
>
> The actual file in the worktree is visited. The positions in the hunk headers get less useful the "older" the changes are, and as a result, jumping to the appropriate position gets less reliable.
>
> Also see `magit-diff-visit-file-worktree`, which visits the respective blob, unless the diff shows changes in the worktree, the index, or **HEAD**.

j   (`magit-jump-to-diffstat-or-diff`)
> Jump to the diffstat or diff. When point is on a file inside the diffstat section, then jump to the respective diff section. Otherwise, jump to the diffstat section or a child thereof.

SPC   (`scroll-up`)
> Scroll text upward.

DEL   (`scroll-down`)
> Scroll text downward.

5.3.3 Diff options

`magit-diff-show-diffstat`   [User Option]
> Whether to show diffstat in diff buffers.

`magit-diff-show-xref-buttons`   [User Option]
>   Whether to show buffer history buttons in diff buffers.

`magit-diff-auto-show`   [User Option]
>   Whether to automatically show the relevant diff or commit.
>
>   When this option is non-nil certain operations cause the relevant changes to be displayed automatically.
>
>   - `commit`
>   - `stage-all`
>   - `log-oneline`
>   - `log-follow`
>   - `log-select`
>   - `blame-follow`
>
>   In the event that expanding very large patches takes a long time, `C-g` can be used to abort that step. This is especially useful when you would normally not look at the changes, e.g. because you are committing some binary files.

`magit-diff-refine-hunk`   [User Option]
>   Whether to show word-granularity differences within diff hunks.
>
>   - `nil` never show fine differences.
>   - `t` show fine differences for the current diff hunk only.
>   - `all` show fine differences for all displayed diff hunks.

`magit-diff-paint-whitespace`   [User Option]
>   Specify where to highlight whitespace errors.
>
>   See `magit-highlight-trailing-whitespace`, `magit-highlight-indentation`. The symbol `t` means in all diffs, `status` means only in the status buffer, and nil means nowhere.

`magit-diff-highlight-trailing`   [User Option]
>   Whether to highlight whitespace at the end of a line in diffs. Used only when `magit-diff-paint-whitespace` is non-nil.

`magit-diff-highlight-indentation`   [User Option]
>   Highlight the "wrong" indentation style. Used only when `magit-diff-paint-whitespace` is non-nil.
>
>   The value is a list of cons cells. The car is a regular expression, and the cdr is the value that applies to repositories whose directory matches the regular expression. If more than one element matches, then the **last** element in the list applies. The default value should therefore come first in the list.
>
>   If the value is `tabs`, highlight indentation with tabs. If the value is an integer, highlight indentation with at least that many spaces. Otherwise, highlight neither.

5.3.4 Revision buffer

`magit-revision-show-diffstat`   [User Option]
    Whether to show diffstat in revision buffers.

`magit-revision-show-notes`   [User Option]
    Whether to show notes in revision buffers.

`magit-revision-show-xref-buttons`   [User Option]
    Whether to show buffer history buttons in revision buffers.

`magit-revision-insert-related-refs`   [User Option]
    Whether to show related refs in revision buffers.

5.4 Ediffing

e   (`magit-ediff-dwim`)
        Compare, stage, or resolve using Ediff.

        This command tries to guess what file, and what commit or range the user
        wants to compare, stage, or resolve using Ediff. It might only be able to guess
        either the file, or range/commit, in which case the user is asked about the other.
        It might not always guess right, in which case the appropriate `magit-ediff-*`
        command has to be used explicitly. If it cannot read the user's mind at all,
        then it asks the user for a command to run.

E   (`magit-ediff-popup`)
        This prefix commands shows the following suffix commands in a popup buffer.

E d   (`magit-ediff-compare`)
        Compare two revisions of a file using Ediff, defaulting to the file at point.

E m   (`magit-ediff-resolve`)
        Resolve outstanding conflicts in a file using Ediff, defaulting to the file at point.

        In the rare event that you want to manually resolve all conflicts, including those
        already resolved by Git, use `ediff-merge-revisions-with-ancestor`.

E s   (`magit-ediff-stage`)
        Stage and unstage changes to a file using Ediff, defaulting to the file at point.

5.5 References buffer

y   (`magit-show-refs-popup`)
        List and compare references in a dedicated buffer. By default all refs are com-
        pared with `HEAD`, but with a prefix argument this command instead acts as
        a prefix command and shows the following suffix commands along with the
        appropriate infix arguments in a popup buffer.

y y   (`magit-show-refs-head`)
        List and compare references in a dedicated buffer. Refs are compared with
        `HEAD`.

y c   (`magit-show-refs-current`)

> List and compare references in a dedicated buffer. Refs are compared with the current branch or `HEAD` if it is detached.

y o   (`magit-show-refs`)

> List and compare references in a dedicated buffer. Refs are compared with a branch read from the user.

`magit-refs-show-commit-count`   [User Option]

> Whether to show commit counts in Magit-Refs mode buffers.
>
> - `all` Show counts for branches and tags.
> - `branch` Show counts for branches only.
> - `nil` Never show counts.
>
> The default is `nil` because anything else can be very expensive.

`magit-refs-show-margin`   [User Option]

> Whether to initially show the margin in refs buffers.
>
> When non-nil the committer name and date are initially displayed in the margin of refs buffers. The margin can be shown or hidden in the current buffer using the command `magit-toggle-margin`.

The following variables control how individual refs are displayed. If you change one of these variables (especially the "%c" part), then you should also change the others to keep things aligned. The following %-sequences are supported:

- `%a` Number of commits this ref has over the one we compare to.
- `%b` Number of commits the ref we compare to has over this one.
- `%c` Number of commits this ref has over the one we compare to. For the ref which all other refs are compared this is instead "@", if it is the current branch, or "#" otherwise.
- `%C` For the ref which all other refs are compared this is "@", if it is the current branch, or "#" otherwise. For all other refs " ".
- `%h` Hash of this ref's tip.
- `%m` Commit summary of the tip of this ref.
- `%n` Name of this ref.
- `%u` Upstream of this local branch and additional local vs. upstream information.
- `%U` Upstream of this local branch.

`magit-refs-local-branch-format`   [Variable]

> Format used for local branches in refs buffers.

`magit-refs-remote-branch-format`   [Variable]

> Format used for remote branches in refs buffers.

`magit-refs-tags-format`   [Variable]

> Format used for tags in refs buffers.

`magit-refs-indent-cherry-lines`   [Variable]

> Indentation of cherries in refs buffers. This should be N-1 where N is taken from "%Nc" in the above format strings.

5.5.1 References sections

The contents of references buffers is controlled using the hook `magit-refs-sections-hook`. See Section 4.4.3 [Section hooks], page 13 to learn about such hooks and how to customize them. All of the below functions are members of the default value. Note that it makes much less sense to customize this hook than it does for the respective hook used for the status buffer.

`magit-refs-sections-hook`   [User Option]
> Hook run to insert sections into a references buffer.

`magit-insert-local-branches`   [Function]
> Insert sections showing all local branches.

`magit-insert-remote-branches`   [Function]
> Insert sections showing all remote-tracking branches.

`magit-insert-tags`   [Function]
> Insert sections showing all tags.

5.6 Bisecting

Also see the git-bisect(1) manpage .

B   (`magit-bisect-popup`)
> This prefix commands shows the following suffix commands in a popup buffer.

When bisecting is not in progress, then the popup buffer features the following commands.

B s   (`magit-bisect-start`)
> Start a bisect session.
>
> Bisecting a bug means to find the commit that introduced it. This command starts such a bisect session by asking for a known good and a bad commit.

B u   (`magit-bisect-run`)
> Bisect automatically by running commands after each step.

When bisecting is in progress, then the popup buffer features these commands instead.

B b   (`magit-bisect-bad`)
> Mark the current commit as bad. Use this after you have asserted that the commit does contain the bug in question.

B g   (`magit-bisect-good`)
> Mark the current commit as good. Use this after you have asserted that the commit does not contain the bug in question.

B k   (`magit-bisect-skip`)
> Skip the current commit. Use this if for some reason the current commit is not a good one to test. This command lets Git choose a different one.

B r   (`magit-bisect-reset`)
> After bisecting, cleanup bisection state and return to original `HEAD`.

5.7 Visiting blobs

M-x magit-find-file   (magit-find-file)
> View FILE from REV. Switch to a buffer visiting blob REV:FILE, creating one if none already exists.

M-x magit-find-file-other-window   (magit-find-file-other-window)
> View FILE from REV, in another window. Like `magit-find-file`, but create a new window or reuse an existing one.

5.8 Blaming

Also see the git-blame(1) manpage .

M-x magit-blame   (magit-blame)
> Display edit history of FILE up to REVISION.
>
> Interactively blame the file being visited in the current buffer. If the buffer visits a revision of that file, then blame up to that revision. Otherwise, blame the file's full history, including uncommitted changes.
>
> If Magit-Blame mode is already turned on then blame recursively, by visiting REVISION:FILE (using `magit-find-file`), where revision is the revision before the revision that added the lines at point.
>
> ARGS is a list of additional arguments to pass to `git blame`; only arguments available from `magit-blame-popup` should be used.

M-x magit-blame-popup   (magit-blame-popup)
> By default this behaves just like `magit-blame`. With a prefix argument instead show a popup buffer featuring a few infix arguments and a single suffix command (`magit-blame`).

RET   (magit-show-commit)
> Show the commit at point. If there is no commit at point or with a prefix argument, prompt for a commit.

SPC   (magit-diff-show-or-scroll-up)
> Update the commit or diff buffer for the thing at point.
>
> Either show the commit or stash at point in the appropriate buffer, or if that buffer is already being displayed in the current frame and contains information about that commit or stash, then instead scroll the buffer up. If there is no commit or stash at point, then prompt for a commit.

DEL   (magit-diff-show-or-scroll-down)
> Update the commit or diff buffer for the thing at point.
>
> Either show the commit or stash at point in the appropriate buffer, or if that buffer is already being displayed in the current frame and contains information about that commit or stash, then instead scroll the buffer down. If there is no commit or stash at point, then prompt for a commit.

n   (magit-blame-next-chunk)
> Move to the next chunk.

N   (`magit-blame-next-chunk-same-commit`)
       Move to the next chunk from the same commit.

p   (`magit-blame-previous-chunk`)
       Move to the previous chunk.

P   (`magit-blame-previous-chunk-same-commit`)
       Move to the previous chunk from the same commit.

q   (`magit-blame-quit`)
       Turn off Magit-Blame mode. If the buffer was created during a recursive blame,
       then also kill the buffer.

t   (`magit-blame-toggle-headings`)
       Show or hide blame chunk headings.

`magit-blame-heading-format`   [User Option]
    Format string used for blame headings.

`magit-blame-time-format`   [User Option]
    Format string used for time strings in blame headings.

`magit-blame-show-headings`   [User Option]
    Whether to initially show blame block headings. The headings can also be toggled
    locally using command `magit-blame-toggle-headings`.

`magit-blame-goto-chunk-hook`   [User Option]
    Hook run by `magit-blame-next-chunk` and `magit-blame-previous-chunk`.

6 Manipulating

6.1 Repository setup

M-x magit-init   (`magit-init`)

> Initialize a Git repository, then show its status.
>
> If the directory is below an existing repository, then the user has to confirm that a new one should be created inside. If the directory is the root of the existing repository, then the user has to confirm that it should be reinitialized.

M-x magit-clone   (`magit-clone`)

> Clone a repository. The user is queried for a remote url and a local directory.

6.2 Staging and unstaging

Like Git, Magit can of course stage and unstage complete files. Unlike Git, it also allows users to gracefully un-/stage individual hunks and even just part of a hunk. To stage individual hunks and parts of hunks using Git directly, one has to use the very modal and rather clumsy interface of a `git add --interactive` session.

With Magit, on the other hand, one can un-/stage individual hunks by just moving point into the respective section inside a diff displayed in the status buffer or a separate diff buffer and typing `s` or `u`. To operate on just parts of a hunk, mark the changes that should be un-/staged using the region and then press the same key that would be used to un-/stage. To stage multiple files or hunks at once use a region that starts inside the heading of such a section and ends inside the heading of a sibling section of the same type.

Besides staging and unstaging, Magit also provides several other "apply variants" that can also operate on a file, multiple files at once, a hunk, multiple hunks at once, and on parts of a hunk. These apply variants are described in the next section.

s   (`magit-stage`)

> Add the change at point to the staging area.

S   (`magit-stage-modified`)

> Stage all changes to files modified in the worktree. Stage all new content of tracked files and remove tracked files that no longer exist in the working tree from the index also. With a prefix argument also stage previously untracked (but not ignored) files.

u   (`magit-unstage`)

> Remove the change at point from the staging area.

U   (`magit-reset-index`)

> Reset the index to some commit. The commit is read from the user and defaults to the commit at point. If there is no commit at point, then it defaults to `HEAD`.
>
> So `U RET` with no commit at point does the inverse of `S` (or actually `S yes RET`), i.e. "unstage all staged changes". If you would rather use a command which always does just that, then rebind `U` to `magit-unstage-all`.

M-x magit-unstage-all   (`magit-unstage-all`)

> Remove all changes from the staging area.

6.2.1 Staging from file-visiting buffers

Fine-grained un-/staging has to be done from the status or a diff buffer, but it's also possible to un-/stage all changes made to the file visited in the current buffer right from inside that buffer.

M-x magit-stage-file   (magit-stage-file)

> When invoked inside a file-visiting buffer, then stage all changes to that file. In a Magit buffer, stage the file at point if any. Otherwise prompt for a file to be staged. With a prefix argument always prompt the user for a file, even in a file-visiting buffer or when there is a file section at point.

M-x magit-unstage-file   (magit-unstage-file)

> When invoked inside a file-visiting buffer, then unstage all changes to that file. In a Magit buffer, unstage the file at point if any. Otherwise prompt for a file to be unstaged. With a prefix argument always prompt the user for a file, even in a file-visiting buffer or when there is a file section at point.

6.3 Applying

Magit provides several "apply variants": stage, unstage, discard, reverse, and "regular apply". At least when operating on a hunk they are all implemented using `git apply`, which is why they are called "apply variants".

- Stage. Apply a change from the working tree to the index. The change also remains in the working tree.
- Unstage. Remove a change from the index. The change remains in the working tree.
- Discard. On a staged change, remove it from the working tree and the index. On an unstaged change, remove it from the working tree only.
- Reverse. Reverse a change in the working tree. Both committed and staged changes can be reversed. Unstaged changes cannot be reversed. Discard them instead.
- Apply. Apply a change to the working tree. Both committed and staged changes can be applied. Unstaged changes cannot be applied - as they already have been applied.

The previous section described the staging and unstaging commands. What follows are the commands which implement the remaining apply variants.

a   (magit-apply)

> Apply the change at point to the working tree. With a prefix argument and if necessary, attempt a 3-way merge.

k   (magit-discard)

> Remove the change at point from the working tree.

v   (magit-reverse)

> Reverse the change at point in the working tree.

6.4 Committing

When the user initiates a commit, Magit calls `git commit` without any arguments, so Git has to get it from the user. It creates the file `.git/COMMIT_EDITMSG` and then opens that file in an editor. Magit arranges for that editor to be the Emacsclient. Once the user finishes the editing session, the Emacsclient exits and Git creates the commit using the file's content as message.

6.4.1 Initiating a commit

Also see the git-commit(1) manpage .

c   (magit-commit-popup)

>This prefix commands shows the following suffix commands along with the appropriate infix arguments in a popup buffer.

c c   (magit-commit)

>Create a new commit on HEAD. With a prefix argument amend to the commit at HEAD instead.

c a   (magit-commit-amend)

>Amend the last commit.

c e   (magit-commit-extend)

>Amend the last commit, without editing the message. With a prefix argument change the committer date. The option magit-commit-extend-override-date can be used to inverse the meaning of the prefix argument.

c r   (magit-commit-reword)

>Reword the last commit, ignoring staged changes.

>With a prefix argument change the committer date. The option magit-commit-rewrite-override-date can be used to inverse the meaning of the prefix argument.

>Non-interactively respect the optional OVERRIDE-DATE argument and ignore the option.

c f   (magit-commit-fixup)

>Create a fixup commit. With a prefix argument the target commit has to be confirmed. Otherwise the commit at point may be used without confirmation depending on the value of option magit-commit-squash-confirm.

c F   (magit-commit-instant-fixup)

>Create a fixup commit and instantly rebase.

c s   (magit-commit-squash)

>Create a squash commit. With a prefix argument the target commit has to be confirmed. Otherwise the commit at point may be used without confirmation depending on the value of option magit-commit-squash-confirm.

c S   (magit-commit-instant-squash)

>Create a squash commit and instantly rebase.

magit-commit-ask-to-stage   [User Option]

>Whether to ask to stage everything when committing and nothing is staged.

magit-commit-extend-override-date   [User Option]

>Whether using magit-commit-extend changes the committer date.

`magit-commit-reword-override-date`   [User Option]
>   Whether using `magit-commit-reword` changes the committer date.

`magit-commit-squash-confirm`   [User Option]
>   Whether the commit targeted by squash and fixup has to be confirmed. When non-
>   nil then the commit at point (if any) is used as default choice. Otherwise it has to
>   be confirmed. This option only affects `magit-commit-squash` and `magit-commit-`
>   `fixup`. The "instant" variants always require confirmation because making an error
>   while using those is harder to recover from.

6.4.2 Editing commit messages

After initiating a commit as described in the previous section, two new buffers appear.
One shows the changes that are about to committed, while the other is used to write the
message. All regular editing commands are available in the commit message buffer. This
section only describes the additional commands.

Commit messages are edited in an edit session - in the background Git is waiting for
the editor, in our case the Emacsclient, to save the commit message in a file (in most cases
`.git/COMMIT_EDITMSG`) and then return. If the Emacsclient returns with a non-zero exit
status then Git does not create the commit. So the most important commands are those
for finishing and aborting the commit.

`C-c C-c`   (`with-editor-finish`)
>   Finish the current editing session by returning with exit code 0. Git then creates
>   the commit using the message it finds in the file.

`C-c C-k`   (`with-editor-cancel`)
>   Cancel the current editing session by returning with exit code 1. Git then
>   cancels the commit, but leaves the file untouched.

In additon to being used by Git, these messages may also be stored in a ring that persists
until Emacs is closed. By default the message is stored at the beginning and the end of an
edit session (regardless of whether the session is finished successfully or was canceled). It
is sometimes useful to bring back messages from that ring.

`C-s M-s`   (`git-commit-save-message`)
>   Save the current buffer content to the commit message ring.

`M-p`   (`git-commit-prev-message`)
>   Cycle backward through the commit message ring, after saving the current
>   message to the ring. With a numeric prefix ARG, go back ARG comments.

`M-n`   (`git-commit-next-message`)
>   Cycle forward through the commit message ring, after saving the current mes-
>   sage to the ring. With a numeric prefix ARG, go back ARG comments.

By default the diff for the changes that are about to be committed are automatically
shown when invoking the commit. When amending to an existing commit it may be useful
to show either the changes that are about to be added to that commit or to show those
changes together with those that are already committed.

C-c C-d   (magit-diff-while-committing)
>   While committing, show the changes that are about to be committed. While
>   amending, invoking the command again toggles between showing just the new
>   changes or all the changes that will be committed.

Some projects use pseudo headers in commit messages. Magit colorizes such headers
and provides some commands to insert such headers.

git-commit-known-pseudo-headers   [User Option]
>   A list of Git pseudo headers to be highlighted.

C-c C-a   (git-commit-ack)
>   Insert a header acknowledging that you have looked at the commit.

C-c C-r   (git-commit-review)
>   Insert a header acknowledging that you have reviewed the commit.

C-c C-s   (git-commit-signoff)
>   Insert a header to sign off the commit.

C-c C-t   (git-commit-test)
>   Insert a header acknowledging that you have tested the commit.

C-c C-o   (git-commit-cc)
>   Insert a header mentioning someone who might be interested.

C-c C-p   (git-commit-reported)
>   Insert a header mentioning the person who reported the issue being fixed by
>   the commit.

C-c C-i   (git-commit-suggested)
>   Insert a header mentioning the person who suggested the change.

git-commit-mode is a minor mode that is only used to establish the above key bindings.
This allows using an arbitrary major mode when editing the commit message. It's even
possible to use a different major mode in different repositories, which is useful when different
projects impose different commit message conventions.

git-commit-major-mode   [User Option]
>   The value of this option is the major mode used to edit Git commit messages.

Because git-commit-mode is a minor mode, we don't use its mode hook to setup the
buffer, except for the key bindings. All other setup happens in the function git-commit-
setup, which among other things runs the hook git-commit-setup-hook. The following
functions are suitable for that hook.

git-commit-setup-hook   [User Option]
>   Hook run at the end of git-commit-setup.

magit-revert-buffers &optional *force*   [Function]
>   Revert unmodified file-visiting buffers of the current repository.
>
>   If either magit-revert-buffers is non-nil and inhibit-magit-revert is nil, or if
>   optional FORCE is non-nil, then revert all unmodified buffers that visit files being
>   tracked in the current repository.

`git-commit-save-message`   [Function]

> Save the current buffer content to the commit message ring.

`git-commit-setup-changelog-support`   [Function]

> After this function is called, ChangeLog entries are treated as paragraphs.

`git-commit-turn-on-auto-fill`   [Function]

> Turn on `auto-fill-mode` and set `fill-column` to the value of `git-commit-fill-column`.

`git-commit-turn-on-flyspell`   [Function]

> Turn on Flyspell mode. Also prevent comments from being checked and finally check current non-comment text.

`git-commit-propertize-diff`   [Function]

> Propertize the diff shown inside the commit message buffer. Git inserts such diffs into the commit message template when the `--verbose` argument is used. Magit's commit popup by default does not offer that argument because the diff that is shown in a separate buffer is more useful. But some users disagree, which is why this function exists.

`with-editor-usage-message`   [Function]

> Show usage information in the echo area.

Magit also helps with writing **good** commit messages by complaining when certain rules are violated.

`git-commit-summary-max-length`   [User Option]

> The intended maximal length of the summary line of commit messages. Characters beyond this column are colorized to indicate that this preference has been violated.

`git-commit-fill-column`   [User Option]

> Column beyond which automatic line-wrapping should happen in commit message buffers.

`git-commit-finish-query-functions`   [User Option]

> List of functions called to query before performing commit.
>
> The commit message buffer is current while the functions are called. If any of them returns nil, then the commit is not performed and the buffer is not killed. The user should then fix the issue and try again.
>
> The functions are called with one argument. If it is non-nil then that indicates that the user used a prefix argument to force finishing the session despite issues. Functions should usually honor this wish and return non-nil.

`git-commit-check-style-conventions`   [Function]

> Check for violations of certain basic style conventions. For each violation ask the user if she wants to proceed anyway. This makes sure the summary line isn't too long and that the second line is empty.

To show no diff while committing remove `magit-commit-diff` from `server-switch-hook`.

6.5 Branching

Also see the git-branch(1) manpage and the git-checkout(1) manpage .

b   (`magit-branch-popup`)

This prefix commands shows the following suffix commands along with the appropriate infix arguments in a popup buffer.

b b   (`magit-checkout`)

Checkout a revision read in the minibuffer and defaulting to the branch or arbitrary revision at point. If the revision is a local branch then that becomes the current branch. If it is something else then `HEAD` becomes detached. Checkout fails if the working tree or the staging area contain changes.

b c   (`magit-branch`)

Create a new branch. The user is asked for a branch or arbitrary revision to use as the starting point of the new branch. When a branch name is provided, then that becomes the upstream branch of the new branch. The name of the new branch is also read in the minibuffer.

b B   (`magit-branch-and-checkout`)

This command creates a new branch like `magit-branch`, but then also checks it out.

b d   (`magit-branch-delete`)

Delete one or multiple branches. If the region marks multiple branches, then offer to delete those. Otherwise, prompt for a single branch to be deleted, defaulting to the branch at point.

b u   (`magit-branch-set-upstream`)

Change the upstream branch of a branch. Both branches are read in the minibuffer, while providing reasonable defaults.

b U   (`magit-branch-unset-upstream`)

Unset the upstream branch of a branch read in the minibuffer and defaulting to the branch at point or the current branch.

b r   (`magit-branch-rename`)

Rename a branch. The branch and the new name are read in the minibuffer. With prefix argument the branch is renamed even if that name conflicts with an existing branch.

b e   (`magit-branch-edit-description`)

Edit the description of a branch. The branch is read in the minibuffer defaulting to the branch at point or the current branch. The description is edited in a regular buffer similar to how commit messages are edited.

6.6 Merging

Also see the git-merge(1) manpage .

m   (`magit-merge-popup`)

This prefix commands shows the following suffix commands along with the appropriate infix arguments in a popup buffer.

When no merge is in progress, then the popup buffer features the following commands.

m m   (`magit-merge`)

> Merge another branch or an arbitrary revision into the current branch. The branch or revision to be merged is read in the minibuffer and defaults to the one at point.
>
> Unless there are conflicts or a prefix argument is used, the resulting merge commit uses a generic commit message, and the user does not get a chance to inspect or change it before the commit is created. With a prefix argument this does not actually create the merge commit, which makes it possible to inspect how conflicts were resolved and to adjust the commit message.

m e   (`magit-merge-editmsg`)

> Merge another branch or an arbitrary revision into the current branch and open a commit message buffer, so that the user can make adjustments. The commit is not actually created until the user finishes with C-c C-c.

m n   (`magit-merge-nocommit`)

> Merge another branch or an arbitrary revision into the current branch, but do not actually create the commit. The user can then further adjust the merge, even when automatic conflict resolution succeeded and/or adjust the commit message.

m p   (`magit-merge-preview`)

> Preview result of merging another branch or an arbitrary revision into the current branch.

When a merge is in progress, then the popup buffer features these commands instead.

m m   (`magit-merge`)

> After resolving conflicts, proceed with the merge. If there are still conflicts, then this fails.

m a   (`magit-merge-abort`)

> Abort the current merge operation.

6.7 Rebasing

Also see the git-rebase(1) manpage .

r   (`magit-rebase-popup`)

> This prefix commands shows the following suffix commands along with the appropriate infix arguments in a popup buffer.

When no rebase is in progress, then the popup buffer features the following commands.

r r   (`magit-rebase`)

> Start a non-interactive rebase sequence. All commits not in UPSTREAM are rebased.

r o   (`magit-rebase-from`)

> Start a non-interactive rebase sequence with commits from START to HEAD onto NEWBASE. START has to be selected from a list of recent commits.

r e   (magit-rebase-interactive)
> Start an interactive rebase sequence.

r f   (magit-rebase-autosquash)
> Combine squash and fixup commits with their intended targets.

r s   (magit-rebase-edit-commit)
> Edit a single older commit using rebase.

r w   (magit-rebase-reword-commit)
> Reword a single older commit using rebase.

When a rebase is in progress, then the popup buffer features these commands instead.

r r   (magit-rebase-continue)
> Restart the current rebasing operation.

r s   (magit-rebase-skip)
> Skip the current commit and restart the current rebase operation.

r e   (magit-rebase-edit)
> Edit the todo list of the current rebase operation.

r a   (magit-rebase-abort)
> Abort the current rebase operation, restoring the original branch.

6.7.1 Editing rebase sequences

C-c C-c   (with-editor-finish)
> Finish the current editing session by returning with exit code 0. Git then creates the commit using the message it finds in the file.

C-c C-k   (with-editor-cancel)
> Cancel the current editing session by returning with exit code 1. Git then cancels the commit, but leaves the file untouched.

RET   (git-rebase-show-commit)
> Show the commit on the current line if any.

p   (git-rebase-backward-line)
> Move to previous line.

n   (forward-line)
> Move to next line.

M-p   (git-rebase-move-line-up)
> Move the current commit (or command) up.

M-n   (git-rebase-move-line-down)
> Move the current commit (or command) down.

r   (git-rebase-reword)
> Edit message of commit on current line.

e   (git-rebase-edit)
> Stop at the commit on the current line.

s   (git-rebase-squash)
>   Meld commit on current line into previous commit, and edit message.

f   (git-rebase-fixup)
>   Meld commit on current line into previous commit, discarding the current commit's message.

k   (git-rebase-kill-line)
>   Kill the current action line.

c   (git-rebase-pick)
>   Use commit on current line.

x   (git-rebase-exec)
>   Insert a shell command to be run after the proceeding commit.
>
>   If there already is such a command on the current line, then edit that instead. With a prefix argument insert a new command even when there already is one on the current line. With empty input remove the command on the current line, if any.

y   (git-rebase-insert)
>   Read an arbitrary commit and insert it below current line.

C-x u   (git-rebase-undo)
>   Undo some previous changes. Like undo but works in read-only buffers.

git-rebase-auto-advance   [User Option]
>   Whether to move to next line after changing a line.

git-rebase-show-instructions   [User Option]
>   Whether to show usage instructions inside the rebase buffer.

git-rebase-confirm-cancel   [User Option]
>   Whether confirmation is required to cancel.

6.8 Cherry picking

Also see the git-cherry-pick(1) manpage .

A   (magit-cherry-pick-popup)
>   This prefix commands shows the following suffix commands along with the appropriate infix arguments in a popup buffer.

   When no cherry-pick or revert is in progress, then the popup buffer features the following commands.

A A   (magit-cherry-pick)
>   Cherry-pick a commit. Prompt for a commit, defaulting to the commit at point. If the region selects multiple commits, then pick all of them, without prompting.

A a   (magit-cherry-apply)
>   Apply the changes in a commit to the working tree, but do not commit them. Prompt for a commit, defaulting to the commit at point. If the region selects multiple commits, then apply all of them, without prompting.

This command also has a top-level binding, which can be invoked without using the popup by typing `a` at the top-level.

When a cherry-pick or revert is in progress, then the popup buffer features these commands instead.

A A   (`magit-sequence-continue`)

> Resume the current cherry-pick or revert sequence.

A s   (`magit-sequence-skip`)

> Skip the stopped at commit during a cherry-pick or revert sequence.

A a   (`magit-sequence-abort`)

> Abort the current cherry-pick or revert sequence. This discards all changes made since the sequence started.

6.8.1 Reverting

V   (`magit-revert-popup`)

> This prefix commands shows the following suffix commands along with the appropriate infix arguments in a popup buffer.

When no cherry-pick or revert is in progress, then the popup buffer features the following commands.

V V   (`magit-revert`)

> Revert a commit by creating a new commit. Prompt for a commit, defaulting to the commit at point. If the region selects multiple commits, then revert all of them, without prompting.

V v   (`magit-revert-no-commit`)

> Revert a commit by applying it in reverse to the working tree. Prompt for a commit, defaulting to the commit at point. If the region selects multiple commits, then revert all of them, without prompting.

When a cherry-pick or revert is in progress, then the popup buffer features these commands instead.

V A   (`magit-sequence-continue`)

> Resume the current cherry-pick or revert sequence.

V s   (`magit-sequence-skip`)

> Skip the stopped at commit during a cherry-pick or revert sequence.

V a   (`magit-sequence-abort`)

> Abort the current cherry-pick or revert sequence. This discards all changes made since the sequence started.

6.9 Resetting

Also see the git-reset(1) manpage .

x   (`magit-reset`)

> Reset the head and index to some commit read from the user and defaulting to the commit at point. The working tree is kept as-is. With a prefix argument also reset the working tree.

U   (`magit-reset-index`)

>   Reset the index to some commit read from the user and defaulting to the commit at point. Keep the `HEAD` and working tree as-is, so if the commit refers to the `HEAD`, then this effectively unstages all changes.

M-x magit-reset-head   (`magit-reset-head`)

>   Reset the `HEAD` and index to some commit read from the user and defaulting to the commit at point. The working tree is kept as-is.

M-x magit-reset-soft   (`magit-reset-soft`)

>   Reset the `HEAD` to some commit read from the user and defaulting to the commit at point. The index and the working tree are kept as-is.

M-x magit-reset-hard   (`magit-reset-hard`)

>   Reset the `HEAD`, index, and working tree to some commit read from the user and defaulting to the commit at point.

6.10 Stashing

Also see the git-stash(1) manpage .

z   (`magit-stash-popup`)

>   This prefix commands shows the following suffix commands along with the appropriate infix arguments in a popup buffer.

z z   (`magit-stash`)

>   Create a stash of the index and working tree. Untracked files are included according to popup arguments. One prefix argument is equivalent to `--include-untracked` while two prefix arguments are equivalent to `--all`.

z i   (`magit-stash-index`)

>   Create a stash of the index only. Unstaged and untracked changes are not stashed.

z w   (`magit-stash-worktree`)

>   Create a stash of the working tree only. Untracked files are included according to popup arguments. One prefix argument is equivalent to `--include-untracked` while two prefix arguments are equivalent to `--all`.

z x   (`magit-stash-keep-index`)

>   Create a stash of the index and working tree, keeping index intact. Untracked files are included according to popup arguments. One prefix argument is equivalent to `--include-untracked` while two prefix arguments are equivalent to `--all`.

z Z   (`magit-snapshot`)

>   Create a snapshot of the index and working tree. Untracked files are included according to popup arguments. One prefix argument is equivalent to `--include-untracked` while two prefix arguments are equivalent to `--all`.

z I   (`magit-snapshot-index`)

>   Create a snapshot of the index only. Unstaged and untracked changes are not stashed.

z W   (`magit-snapshot-worktree`)

   Create a snapshot of the working tree only. Untracked files are included according to popup arguments. One prefix argument is equivalent to `--include-untracked` while two prefix arguments are equivalent to `--all-`.

z a   (`magit-stash-apply`)

   Apply a stash to the working tree. Try to preserve the stash index. If that fails because there are staged changes, apply without preserving the stash index.

z p   (`magit-stash-pop`)

   Apply a stash to the working tree and remove it from stash list. Try to preserve the stash index. If that fails because there are staged changes, apply without preserving the stash index and forgo removing the stash.

z d   (`magit-stash-drop`)

   Remove a stash from the stash list. When the region is active, offer to drop all contained stashes.

z l   (`magit-stash-list`)

   List all stashes in a buffer.

z v   (`magit-stash-show`)

   Show all diffs of a stash in a buffer.

z b   (`magit-stash-branch`)

   Create and checkout a new BRANCH from STASH.

k   (`magit-stash-clear`)

   Remove all stashes saved in REF's reflog by deleting REF.

7 Transferring

7.1 Remotes

Also see the git-remote(1) manpage .

M   (magit-remote-popup)
> This prefix commands shows the following suffix commands along with the appropriate infix arguments in a popup buffer.

M a   (magit-remote-add)
> Add a remote and fetch it. The remote name and url are read in the minibuffer.

M r   (magit-remote-rename)
> Rename a remote. Both the old and the new names are read in the minibuffer.

M u   (magit-remote-set-url)
> Change the url of a remote. Both the remote and the new url are read in the minibuffer.

M k   (magit-remote-remove)
> Delete a remote, read from the minibuffer.

7.2 Fetching

Also see the git-fetch(1) manpage .

f   (magit-fetch-popup)
> This prefix commands shows the following suffix commands along with the appropriate infix arguments in a popup buffer.

f f   (magit-fetch-current)
> Fetch from the upstream repository of the current branch. If HEAD is detached or if the upstream is not configured, then read the remote.

f o   (magit-fetch)
> Fetch from another repository.

f a   (magit-fetch-all)
> Fetch from all configured remotes.

f m   (magit-submodule-fetch)
> Fetch all submodules. With a prefix argument fetch all remotes or all submodules.

7.3 Pulling

Also see the git-pull(1) manpage .

F   (magit-pull-popup)
> This prefix commands shows the following suffix commands along with the appropriate infix arguments in a popup buffer.

F F   (magit-pull-current)
> Fetch and merge into current branch.

F o   (magit-pull)
>   Fetch from another repository and merge a fetched branch.

7.4 Pushing

Also see the git-push(1) manpage .

P   (magit-push-popup)
>   This prefix commands shows the following suffix commands along with the
>   appropriate infix arguments in a popup buffer.

P P   (magit-push-current)
>   Push the current branch to its upstream branch. If the upstream isn't set, then
>   read the remote branch.

P o   (magit-push)
>   Push a branch to its upstream branch. If the upstream isn't set, then read the
>   remote branch.

P e   (magit-push-elsewhere)
>   Push a branch or commit to some remote branch. Read the local and remote
>   branch.

P m   (magit-push-matching)
>   Push all matching branches to another repository. If multiple remotes exit,
>   then read one from the user. If just one exists, use that without requiring
>   confirmation.

P t   (magit-push-tags)
>   Push all tags to another repository. If only one remote exists, then push to
>   that. Otherwise prompt for a remote, offering the remote configured for the
>   current branch as default.

P T   (magit-push-tag)
>   Push a tag to another repository.

7.5 Creating and sending patches

W   (magit-patch-popup)
>   This prefix commands shows the following suffix commands along with the
>   appropriate infix arguments in a popup buffer.

W p   (magit-format-patch)
>   Create patches for a set commits. If the region marks commits, then create
>   patches for those. Otherwise prompt for a range or a single commit, defaulting
>   to the commit at point.

W r   (magit-request-pull)
>   Request that upstream pulls from your public repository.

7.6 Applying patches

Also see the git-am(1) manpage .

w   (magit-am-popup)
        This prefix commands shows the following suffix commands along with the
        appropriate infix arguments in a popup buffer.

w w   (magit-am-apply-patches)
        Apply one or more patches. If the region marks files, then apply those patches.
        Otherwise read a file name in the minibuffer defaulting to the file at point.

w m   (magit-am-apply-maildir)
        Apply the patches from a maildir.

w w   (magit-am-continue)
        Resume the current patch applying sequence.

w s   (magit-am-skip)
        Skip the stopped at patch during a patch applying sequence.

w a   (magit-am-abort)
        Abort the current patch applying sequence. This discards all changes made
        since the sequence started.

8 Miscellaneous

8.1 Tagging

Also see the git-tag(1) manpage .

t   (`magit-tag-popup`)
>   This prefix commands shows the following suffix commands along with the
>   appropriate infix arguments in a popup buffer.

t t   (`magit-tag`)
>   Create a new tag with the given NAME at REV. With a prefix argument
>   annotate the tag.

t k   (`magit-tag-delete`)
>   Delete one or more tags. If the region marks multiple tags (and nothing else),
>   then offer to delete those. Otherwise, prompt for a single tag to be deleted,
>   defaulting to the tag at point.

t p   (`magit-tag-prune`)
>   Offer to delete tags missing locally from REMOTE, and vice versa.

8.2 Notes

Also see the git-notes(1) manpage .

T   (`magit-notes-popup`)
>   This prefix commands shows the following suffix commands along with the
>   appropriate infix arguments in a popup buffer.

T T   (`magit-notes-edit`)
>   Edit the note attached to a commit, defaulting to the commit at point.
>
>   By default use the value of Git variable `core.notesRef` or
>   "refs/notes/commits" if that is undefined.

T r   (`magit-notes-remove`)
>   Remove the note attached to a commit, defaulting to the commit at point.
>
>   By default use the value of Git variable `core.notesRef` or
>   "refs/notes/commits" if that is undefined.

T p   (`magit-notes-prune`)
>   Remove notes about unreachable commits.

T s   (`magit-notes-set-ref`)
>   Set the current notes ref to a the value read from the user. The ref is made
>   current by setting the value of the Git variable `core.notesRef`. With a prefix
>   argument change the global value instead of the value in the current repository.
>   When this is undefined, then "refs/notes/commit" is used.
>
>   Other `magit-notes-*` commands, as well as the sub-commands of Git's `note`
>   command, default to operate on that ref.

T S (`magit-notes-set-display-refs`)
> Set notes refs to be display in addition to "core.notesRef". This reads a colon separated list of notes refs from the user. The values are stored in the Git variable `notes.displayRef`. With a prefix argument GLOBAL change the global values instead of the values in the current repository.

It is possible to merge one note ref into another. That may result in conflicts which have to resolved in the temporary worktree ".git/$NOTES_{MERGE}WORKTREE$".

T m (`magit-notes-merge`)
> Merge the notes of a ref read from the user into the current notes ref. The current notes ref is the value of Git variable `core.notesRef` or "refs/notes/commits" if that is undefined.

When a notes merge is in progress then the popup features the following suffix commands, instead of those listed above.

T c (`magit-notes-merge-commit`)
> Commit the current notes ref merge, after manually resolving conflicts.

T a (`magit-notes-merge-abort`)
> Abort the current notes ref merge.

8.3 Submodules

Also see the git-submodule(1) manpage .

o (`magit-submodule-popup`)
> This prefix commands shows the following suffix commands along with the appropriate infix arguments in a popup buffer.

o a (`magit-submodule-add`)
> Add the repository at URL as a submodule. Optional PATH is the path to the submodule relative to the root of the super-project. If it is nil then the path is determined based on URL.

o b (`magit-submodule-setup`)
> Clone and register missing submodules and checkout appropriate commits.

o i (`magit-submodule-init`)
> Register submodules listed in ".gitmodules" into ".git/config".

o u (`magit-submodule-update`)
> Clone missing submodules and checkout appropriate commits. With a prefix argument also register submodules in ".git/config".

o s (`magit-submodule-sync`)
> Update each submodule's remote URL according to ".gitmodules".

o f (`magit-submodule-fetch`)
> Fetch submodule. With a prefix argument fetch all remotes.

8.4 Wip Modes

Git keeps **committed** changes around long enough for users to recover changes they have accidentally deleted. It does so by not garbage collecting any committed but no longer referenced objects for a certain period of time, by default 30 days.

But Git does **not** keep track of **uncommitted** changes in the working tree and not even the index (the staging area). Because Magit makes it so convenient to modify uncommitted changes, it also makes it easy to shoot yourself in the foot in the process.

For that reason Magit provides three global modes that save **tracked** files to work-in-progress references after or before certain actions. (Untracked files are never saved and these modes also only work after the first commit has been created).

Two separate work-in-progress references are used to track the state of the index and of the working tree: "refs/wip/index/<branchref>" and "refs/wip/wtree/<branchref>", where <branchref> is the full ref of the current branch, e.g. "refs/heads/master". When the HEAD is detached then "HEAD" is in place of <branchref>.

Checking out another branch (or detaching HEAD) causes the use of different wip refs for subsequent changes, but the old refs are not deleted.

Creating a commit and then making a change causes the wip refs to be recreated to fork from the new commit. But the old commits on the wip refs are not lost. They are still available from the reflog. To make it easier to see when the fork point of a wip ref was changed, an additional commit with the message "restart autosaving" is created on it (xx0 commits below are such boundary commits).

Starting with

```
    BI0---BI1      refs/wip/index/refs/heads/master
   /
A---B              refs/heads/master
   \
    BW0---BW1      refs/wip/wtree/refs/heads/master
```

and committing the staged changes and editing and saving a file would result in

```
    BI0---BI1          refs/wip/index/refs/heads/master
   /
A---B---C              refs/heads/master
   \   \
    \   CW0---CW1      refs/wip/wtree/refs/heads/master
     \
      BW0---BW1        refs/wip/wtree/refs/heads/master@{2}
```

The fork-point of the index wip ref is not changed until some change is being staged. Likewise just checking out a branch or creating a commit does not change the fork-point of the working tree wip ref. The fork-points are not adjusted until there actually is a change that should be committed to the respective wip ref.

To recover a lost change from a wip ref, use the reflog. To show the reflog, use e.g. `l O refs/wip/index/refs/heads/master` RET and then move around until you find the commit which has the lost change. You might then be able to simply apply it using `a` (`magit-apply`).

There exists a total of three global modes that save to the wip refs, which might seem excessive, but allows fine tuning of when exactly changes are being committed to the wip refs. Enabling all modes makes it less likely that a change slips through the cracks.

`magit-wip-after-save-mode`   [User Option]

When this mode is enabled, then saving a buffer that visits a file tracked in a Git repository causes its current state to be committed to the working tree wip ref for the current branch.

`magit-wip-after-apply-mode`   [User Option]

When this mode is enabled, then applying (i.e. staging, unstaging, discarding, reversing, and regularly applying) a change to a file tracked in a Git repository causes its current state to be committed to the index and/or working tree wip refs for the current branch.

If you only ever edit files using Emacs and only ever interact with Git using Magit, then the above two modes should be enough to protect each and every change from accidental loss. In practice nobody does that. So an additional mode exists that does commit to the wip refs before making changes that could cause the loss of earlier changes.

`magit-wip-before-change-mode`   [User Option]

When this mode is enabled, then certain commands commit the existing changes to the files they are about to make changes to.

Note that even if you enable all three modes this won't give you perfect protection. The most likely scenario for losing changes despite the use of these modes is making a change outside Emacs and then destroying it also outside Emacs. In such a scenario, Magit, being an Emacs package, didn't get the opportunity to keep you from shooting yourself in the foot.

When you are unsure whether Magit did commit a change to the wip refs, then you can explicitly request that all changes to all tracked files are being committed.

M-x magit-wip-commit   (`magit-wip-commit`)

This command commits all changes to all tracked files to the index and working tree work-in-progress refs. Like the modes described above, it does not commit untracked files, but it does check all tracked files for changes. Use this command when you suspect that the modes might have overlooked a change made outside Emacs/Magit.

`magit-wip-after-save-local-mode-lighter`   [User Option]

Mode-line lighter for `magit-wip-after-save-local-mode`.

`magit-wip-after-apply-mode-lighter`   [User Option]

Mode-line lighter for `magit-wip-after-apply-mode`.

`magit-wip-before-change-mode-lighter`   [User Option]

Mode-line lighter for `magit-wip-before-change-mode`.

`magit-wip-namespace`   [User Option]

The namespace used for work-in-progress refs. It has to end with a slash. The wip refs are named "<namespace>index/<branchref>" and "<namespace>wtree/<branchref>".

When snapshots are created while the `HEAD` is detached then "HEAD" is used in place of `<branchref>`.

9 Customizing

Both Git and Emacs are highly customizable. Magit is both a Git porcelain as well as an Emacs package, so it makes sense to customize it using both Git variables as well as Emacs options. However this flexibility doesn't come without problems, including but not limited to the following.

- Some Git variables automatically have an effect in Magit without requiring any explicit support. Sometimes that is desirable - in other cases, it breaks Magit.

  When a certain Git setting breaks Magit but you want to keep using that setting on the command line, then that can be accomplished by overriding the value for Magit only by appending something like ("-c" "some.variable=compatible-value") to `magit-git-global-arguments`.

- Certain settings like `fetch.prune=true` are respected by Magit commands (because they simply call the respective Git command) but their value is not reflected in the respective popup buffers. In this case the `--prune` argument in `magit-fetch-popup` might be active or inactive depending on the value of `magit-fetch-arguments` only, but that doesn't keep the Git variable from being honored by the suffix commands anyway. So pruning might happen despite the the `--prune` arguments being displayed in a way that seems to indicate that no pruning will happen.

I intend to address these and similar issues in a future release.

9.1 Per-repository configuration

Magit can be configured on a per-repository level using both Git variables as well as Emacs options.

To set a Git variable for one repository only, simply set it in `/path/to/repo/.git/config` instead of `$HOME/.gitconfig` or `/etc/gitconfig`. See the git-config(1) manpage .

Similarly, Emacs options can be set for one repository only by editing `/path/to/repo/.dir-locals.el`. See Section "Directory Variables" in emacs. For example to disable automatic refreshes of file-visiting buffers in just one huge repository use this:

- `/path/to/huge/repo/.dir-locals.el`

      ((nil . ((magit-refresh-buffers . nil))

If you want to apply the same settings to several, but not all, repositories then keeping the repository-local config files in sync would quickly become annoying. To avoid that you can create config files for certain classes of repositories (e.g. "huge repositories") and then include those files in the per-repository config files. For example:

- `/path/to/huge/repo/.git/config`

      [include]
              path = /path/to/huge-gitconfig

- `/path/to/huge-gitconfig`

      [status]
              showUntrackedFiles = no

- `$HOME/.emacs.d/init.el`

```
(dir-locals-set-class-variables 'huge-git-repository
   '((nil . ((magit-refresh-buffers . nil)))))

(dir-locals-set-directory-class
   "/path/to/huge/repo/" 'huge-git-repository)
```

9.2 Essential settings

The next two sections list and discuss several variables that many users might want to customize, for safety and/or performance reasons.

9.2.1 Safety

This section discusses various variables that you might want to change (or **not** change) for safety reasons.

Git keeps **committed** changes around long enough for users to recover changes they have accidentally deleted. It does not do the same for **uncommitted** changes in the working tree and not even the index (the staging area). Because Magit makes it so easy to modify uncommitted changes, it also makes it easy to shoot yourself in the foot in the process. For that reason Magit provides three global modes that save **tracked** files to work-in-progress references after or before certain actions. See Section 8.4 [Wip Modes], page 51.

These modes are not enabled by default because of performance concerns. Instead a lot of potentially destructive commands require confirmation every time they are used. In many cases this can be disabled by adding a symbol to **magit-no-confirm** (see Section 4.6 [Completion and confirmation], page 14). If you enable the various wip modes then you should add **safe-with-wip** to this list.

Similarly it isn't necessary to require confirmation before moving a file to the system trash - if you trashed a file by mistake then you can recover it from the there. Option **magit-delete-by-moving-to-trash** controls whether the system trash is used, which is the case by default. Nevertheless, **trash** isn't a member of **magit-no-confirm** - you might want to change that.

Buffers visiting files tracked in the current repository are being refreshed before certain actions. See Section 4.3 [Automatic refresh and revert], page 9. This isn't as risky as it might seem. If a buffer is modified (i.e. it contains changes that haven't been saved yet), then Emacs/Magit would refuse to revert it. If the buffer has been saved resulting in what is seen by Git as an uncommitted change, then Git in turn would refuse to carry out the action that would cause these changes to be lost. Since Git doesn't do anything, the file doesn't change on disk, and Emacs/Magit has nothing to revert.

However if you do modify some files, visit the respective files in Emacs, somehow discard the changes (not using Magit and probably even outside Emacs), and then expect the respective file-visiting buffers to retain the uncommitted changes, then the automatic reverting would actually be harmful. In other words if you use file-visiting buffers as a sort of "staging area", then you should set **magit-revert-buffers** to **nil**.

So far I have only heard from one user who uses such a workflow. But because there might be some other users doing such things, and I don't want to be responsible for data loss, these reverts by default happen quite verbosely, allowing these few users to undo the reverts using the **undo** command and then disabling the automatic reverts for the future.

Most users should however keep automatic reverts turned on and instead configure it to be less verbose by setting `magit-revert-buffers` to `t` or even `silent`.

9.2.2 Performance

Magit is slower than raw Git because it does more. For example `git commit` creates a commit and that's it. `magit-commit` also updates the current Magit buffer to make sure you are not looking at outdated information without noticing it. To refresh the status buffer, Magit has to run Git a dozen times or more, making it slower than `git status`, but also much more informative. Magit also optionally reverts file-visiting buffers, creates backups, runs hooks where third-party extensions can do their slow thing, etc.

I do care about performance and try to optimize for it as much as possible, but many features simply come with an inherent performance penalty. When a feature is just too slow given certain usage and repository characteristics, then it often can be disabled, globally or on a per-repository basis.

But first a short list of performance issues that cannot easily be worked around:

- Creating a new process on MS Windows is much slower than on POSIX-compatible systems. This is a problem because Magit creates a lot of child processes to retrieve information from Git. In the short run, only switching to a POSIX system can fix this. Of course this could also be fixed in Windows itself, but I am just one unpaid person while Microsoft is a billion dollar company, so I will leave it to them to fix this grave flaw in their OS.

- When showing logs, Magit limits the number of commits initially shown in the hope that this avoids unnecessary work. When using `--graph` this unfortunately does not have the desired effect for large histories. Junio said on the git mailing list (`http://www.spinics.net/lists/git/msg232230.html`): "`--graph` wants to compute the whole history and the max-count only affects the output phase after `--graph` does its computation".

  In other words, it's not that Git is slow at outputting the differences, or that Magit is slow at parsing the output - the problem is that Git first goes outside and has a smoke. This has to be fixed in Git but so far nobody volunteered to do it. Maybe you could do that?

- Whenever "something changes", Magit "refreshes" the status buffer and the current Magit buffer by recreating them from scratch. This is an old design decision that we couldn't depart from easily. And it has its benefits too - most importantly it's much simpler and less error prone to do it this way than to only refreshing "what actually has changed" (that would basically be a huge collection of special cases). So for now at least, we don't avoid recreating the buffer content and instead focus on making doing so faster.

Now for the things that you can do to improve performance:

Most optional features which can have a negative effect on performance are disabled by default. So start by checking the options you have customized. Even the potentially slow features are expected to only lead to barely noticeable delays, but your mileage may vary. Also note that it is now possible to set options on a per-repository or per-repository-class basis. See Section 9.1 [Per-repository configuration], page 54.

You should check the values of at least the following variables:

- `magit-after-revert-hook`
- `magit-diff-auto-show`
- `magit-diff-highlight-hunk-body`
- `magit-diff-highlight-indentation`
- `magit-diff-highlight-whitespace`
- `magit-diff-paint-whitespace`
- `magit-diff-refine-hunk`
- `magit-not-reverted-hook`
- `magit-refresh-buffer-hook`
- `magit-status-refresh-hook`
- `magit-wip-after-apply-mode`
- `magit-wip-after-save-mode`
- `magit-wip-before-change-mode`

Also note that everything involving "cherry commits" is slow.

If nothing helps, then feel free to open a new issue. Please provide benchmarks.

10 Plumbing

The following sections describe how to use several of Magit's core abstractions to extend Magit itself or implement a separate extension.

A few of the low-level features used by Magit have been factored out into separate libraries/packages, so that they can be used by other packages, without having to depend on Magit. These libraries are described in separate manuals, see `with-editor` and `magit-popup`.

10.1 Calling Git

Magit provides many specialized functions for calling Git. All of these functions are defined in either `magit-git.el` or `magit-process.el` and have one of the prefixes `magit-run-`, `magit-call-`, `magit-start-`, or `magit-git-` (which is also used for other things).

All of these functions accept an indefinite number of arguments, which are strings that specify command line arguments for git (or in some cases an arbitrary executable). These arguments are flattened before being passed on to the executable; so instead of strings they can also be lists of strings and arguments that are `nil` are silently dropped. Some of these functions also require a single mandatory argument before these command line arguments.

Roughly speaking these functions run Git either to get some value or for side-effect. The functions that return a value are useful to collect the information necessary to populate a Magit buffer, while the others are used to implement Magit commands.

The functions in the value-only group always run synchronously, and they never trigger a refresh. The function in the side-effect group can be further divided into subgroups depending on whether they run Git synchronously or asynchronously, and depending on whether they trigger a refresh when the executable has finished.

10.1.1 Getting a value from Git

These functions run Git in order to get a value, either its exit status or its output. Of course you could also use them to run Git commands that have side-effects, but that should be avoided.

magit-git-exit-code &rest *args*   [Function]
     Executes git with ARGS and returns its exit code.

magit-git-success &rest *args*   [Function]
     Executes git with ARGS and returns t if the exit code is 0, `nil` otherwise.

magit-git-failure &rest *args*   [Function]
     Executes git with ARGS and returns t if the exit code is 1, `nil` otherwise.

magit-git-true &rest *args*   [Function]
     Executes git with ARGS and returns t if the first line printed by git is the string "true", `nil` otherwise.

magit-git-false &rest *args*   [Function]
     Executes git with ARGS and returns t if the first line printed by git is the string "false", `nil` otherwise.

magit-git-insert **&rest** *args*   [Function]
> Executes git with ARGS and inserts its output at point.

magit-git-string **&rest** *args*   [Function]
> Executes git with ARGS and returns the first line of its output. If there is no output
> or if it begins with a newline character, then this returns **nil**.

magit-git-lines **&rest** *args*   [Function]
> Executes git with ARGS and returns its output as a list of lines. Empty lines anywhere
> in the output are omitted.

magit-git-items **&rest** *args*   [Function]
> Executes git with ARGS and returns its null-separated output as a list. Empty items
> anywhere in the output are omitted.
>
> If the value of option **magit-git-debug** is non-nil and git exits with a non-zero exit
> status, then warn about that in the echo area and add a section containing git's
> standard error in the current repository's process buffer.

When an error occurs when using one of the above functions, then that is usually due to
a bug, i.e. the use of an argument which is not actually supported. Such errors are usually
not reported, but when they occur we need to be able to debug them.

magit-git-debug   [User Option]
> Whether to report errors that occur when using **magit-git-insert**, **magit-git-**
> **string**, **magit-git-lines**, or **magit-git-items**. This does not actually raise an
> error. Instead a message is shown in the echo area, and git's standard error is insert
> into a new section in the current repository's process buffer.

magit-git-str **&rest** *args*   [Function]
> This is a variant of **magit-git-string** that ignores the option **magit-git-debug**. It
> is mainly intended to be used while handling errors in functions that do respect that
> option. Using such a function while handing an error could cause yet another error
> and therefore lead to an infinite recursion. You probably won't ever need to use this
> function.

10.1.2 Calling Git for effect

These functions are used to run git to produce some effect. Most Magit commands that
actually run git do so by using such a function.

Because we do not need to consume git's output when using these functions, their output
is instead logged into a per-repository buffer, which can be shown using **$** from a Magit
buffer or **M-x** **magit-process** elsewhere.

These functions can have an effect in two distinct ways. Firstly, running git may change
something, i.e. create or push a new commit. Secondly, that change may require that
Magit buffers are refreshed to reflect the changed state of the repository. But refreshing
isn't always desirable, so only some of these functions do perform such a refresh after git
has returned.

Sometimes it is useful to run git asynchronously. For example, when the user has just
initiated a push, then there is no reason to make her wait until that has completed. In

other cases it makes sense to wait for git to complete before letting the user do something else. For example after staging a change it is useful to wait until after the refresh because that also automatically moves to the next change.

`magit-call-git` **&rest** *args* [Function]
> Calls git synchronously with ARGS.

`magit-call-process` *program* **&rest** *args* [Function]
> Calls PROGRAM synchronously with ARGS.

`magit-run-git` **&rest** *args* [Function]
> Calls git synchronously with ARGS and then refreshes.

`magit-run-git-with-input` *input* **&rest** *args* [Function]
> Calls git synchronously with ARGS and sends it INPUT on standard input.
>
> INPUT should be a buffer or the name of an existing buffer. The content of that buffer is used as the process' standard input. After the process returns a refresh is performed.
>
> As a special case, INPUT may also be nil. In that case the content of the current buffer is used as standard input and **no** refresh is performed.
>
> This function actually runs git asynchronously. But then it waits for the process to return, so the function itself is synchronous.

`magit-run-git-with-logfile` *file* **&rest** *args* [Function]
> Calls git synchronously with ARGS. The process' output is saved in FILE. This is rarely useful and so this function might be removed in the future.
>
> This function actually runs git asynchronously. But then it waits for the process to return, so the function itself is synchronous.

`magit-git` **&rest** *args* [Function]
> Calls git synchronously with ARGS for side-effects only. This function does not refresh the buffer.

`magit-git-wash` *washer* **&rest** *args* [Function]
> Execute Git with ARGS, inserting washed output at point. Actually first insert the raw output at point. If there is no output call `magit-cancel-section`. Otherwise temporarily narrow the buffer to the inserted text, move to its beginning, and then call function WASHER with no argument.

And now for the asynchronous variants.

`magit-run-git-async` **&rest** *args* [Function]
> Start Git, prepare for refresh, and return the process object. ARGS is flattened and then used as arguments to Git.
>
> Display the command line arguments in the echo area.
>
> After Git returns some buffers are refreshed: the buffer that was current when this function was called (if it is a Magit buffer and still alive), as well as the respective Magit status buffer. Unmodified buffers visiting files that are tracked in the current repository are reverted if `magit-revert-buffers` is non-nil.

magit-run-git-with-editor **&rest** *args*   [Function]

> Export GIT$_E DITOR$ and start Git. Also prepare for refresh and return the process object. ARGS is flattened and then used as arguments to Git.
>
> Display the command line arguments in the echo area.
>
> After Git returns some buffers are refreshed: the buffer that was current when this function was called (if it is a Magit buffer and still alive), as well as the respective Magit status buffer.

magit-start-git **&rest** *args*   [Function]

> Start Git, prepare for refresh, and return the process object.
>
> If INPUT is non-nil, it has to be a buffer or the name of an existing buffer. The buffer content becomes the processes standard input.
>
> Option `magit-git-executable` specifies the Git executable and option `magit-git-global-arguments` specifies constant arguments. The remaining arguments ARGS specify arguments to Git. They are flattened before use.
>
> After Git returns, some buffers are refreshed: the buffer that was current when this function was called (if it is a Magit buffer and still alive), as well as the respective Magit status buffer. Unmodified buffers visiting files that are tracked in the current repository are reverted if `magit-revert-buffers` is non-nil.

magit-start-process **&rest** *args*   [Function]

> Start PROGRAM, prepare for refresh, and return the process object.
>
> If optional argument INPUT is non-nil, it has to be a buffer or the name of an existing buffer. The buffer content becomes the processes standard input.
>
> The process is started using `start-file-process` and then setup to use the sentinel `magit-process-sentinel` and the filter `magit-process-filter`. Information required by these functions is stored in the process object. When this function returns the process has not started to run yet so it is possible to override the sentinel and filter.
>
> After the process returns, `magit-process-sentinel` refreshes the buffer that was current when `magit-start-process` was called (if it is a Magit buffer and still alive), as well as the respective Magit status buffer. Unmodified buffers visiting files that are tracked in the current repository are reverted if `magit-revert-buffers` is non-nil.

magit-this-process   [Variable]

> The child process which is about to start. This can be used to change the filter and sentinel.

magit-process-raise-error   [Variable]

> When this is non-nil, then `magit-process-sentinel` raises an error if git exits with a non-zero exit status. For debugging purposes.

10.2 Section plumbing

10.2.1 Creating sections

magit-insert-section **&rest** *args*   [Macro]
> Insert a section at point.

> TYPE is the section type, a symbol. Many commands that act on the current section behave differently depending on that type. Also if a variable `magit-TYPE-section-map` exists, then use that as the text-property `keymap` of all text belonging to the section (but this may be overwritten in subsections).

> Optional VALUE is the value of the section, usually a string that is required when acting on the section.

> When optional HIDE is non-nil collapse the section body by default, i.e. when first creating the section, but not when refreshing the buffer. Otherwise, expand it by default. This can be overwritten using `magit-section-set-visibility-hook`. When a section is recreated during a refresh, then the visibility of predecessor is inherited and HIDE is ignored (but the hook is still honored).

> BODY is any number of forms that actually insert the section's heading and body. Optional NAME, if specified, has to be a symbol, which is then bound to the struct of the section being inserted.

> Before BODY is evaluated the `start` of the section object is set to the value of `point` and after BODY was evaluated its `end` is set to the new value of `point`; BODY is responsible for moving `point` forward.

> If it turns out inside BODY that the section is empty, then `magit-cancel-section` can be used to abort and remove all traces of the partially inserted section. This can happen when creating a section by washing Git's output and Git didn't actually output anything this time around.

magit-insert-heading **&rest** *args*   [Function]
> Insert the heading for the section currently being inserted.

> This function should only be used inside `magit-insert-section`.

> When called without any arguments, then just set the `content` slot of the object representing the section being inserted to a marker at `point`. The section should only contain a single line when this function is used like this.

> When called with arguments ARGS, which have to be strings, then insert those strings at point. The section should not contain any text before this happens and afterwards it should again only contain a single line. If the `face` property is set anywhere inside any of these strings, then insert all of them unchanged. Otherwise use the `magit-section-heading` face for all inserted text.

> The `content` property of the section struct is the end of the heading (which lasts from `start` to `content`) and the beginning of the body (which lasts from `content` to `end`). If the value of `content` is nil, then the section has no heading and its body cannot be collapsed. If a section does have a heading then its height must be exactly one line, including a trailing newline character. This isn't enforced; you are responsible for getting it right. The only exception is that this function does insert a newline character if necessary.

magit-cancel-section   [Function]

> Cancel the section currently being inserted. This exits the innermost call to
> `magit-insert-section` and removes all traces of what has already happened inside
> that call.

magit-define-section-jumper *sym title* **&optional** *value*   [Function]

> Define an interactive function to go to section SYM. TITLE is the displayed title of
> the section.

10.2.2 Section selection

magit-current-section   [Function]

> Return the section at point.

magit-region-sections   [Function]

> Return a list of the selected sections.
>
> When the region is active and constitutes a valid section selection, then return a list
> of all selected sections. This is the case when the region begins in the heading of a
> section and ends in the heading of a sibling of that first section. When the selection
> is not valid then return nil. Most commands that can act on the selected sections,
> then instead just act on the current section, the one point is in.
>
> When the region looks like it would in any other buffer then the selection is invalid.
> When the selection is valid then the region uses the `magit-section-highlight`. This
> does not apply to diffs where things get a bit more complicated, but even here if the
> region looks like it usually does, then that's not a valid selection as far as this function
> is concerned.

magit-region-values **&rest** *types*   [Function]

> Return a list of the values of the selected sections.
>
> Also see `magit-region-sections` whose doc-string explains when a region is a valid
> section selection. If the region is not active or is not a valid section selection, then
> return nil. If optional TYPES is non-nil then the selection not only has to be valid;
> the types of all selected sections additionally have to match one of TYPES, or nil is
> returned.

10.2.3 Matching sections

M-x magit-describe-section   (magit-describe-section)

> Show information about the section at point. This command is intended for
> debugging purposes.

magit-section-ident   [Function]

> Return an unique identifier for SECTION. The return value has the form `((TYPE .`
> `VALUE)...)`.

magit-get-section   [Function]

> Return the section identified by IDENT. IDENT has to be a list as returned by
> `magit-section-ident`.

magit-section-match *condition* **&optional** *section*   [Function]

> Return **t** if SECTION matches CONDITION. SECTION defaults to the section at point.
>
> Conditions can take the following forms:
>
> - (CONDITION...)
>
>   matches if any of the CONDITIONs matches.
>
> - [TYPE...]
>
>   matches if the first TYPE matches the type of the section at point, the second matches that of its parent, and so on.
>
> - [* TYPE...]
>
>   matches sections that match [TYPE...] and also recursively all their child sections.
>
> - TYPE
>
>   matches TYPE regardless of its parents.
>
> Each TYPE is a symbol. Note that is not necessary to specify all TYPEs up to the root section as printed by **magit-describe-type**, unless of course your want to be that precise.

magit-section-when *condition* **&rest** *body*   [Function]

> If the section at point matches CONDITION evaluate BODY.
>
> If the section matches evaluate BODY forms sequentially and return the value of the last one, or if there are no BODY forms return the value of the section. If the section does not match return nil.
>
> See **magit-section-match** for the forms CONDITION can take.

magit-section-case **&rest** *clauses*   [Function]

> Choose among clauses on the type of the section at point.
>
> Each clause looks like (CONDITION BODY...). The type of the section is compared against each CONDITION; the BODY forms of the first match are evaluated sequentially and the value of the last form is returned. Inside BODY the symbol **it** is bound to the section at point. If no clause succeeds or if there is no section at point return nil.
>
> See **magit-section-match** for the forms CONDITION can take. Additionally a CONDITION of t is allowed in the final clause and matches if no other CONDITION match, even if there is no section at point.

magit-root-section   [Variable]

> The root section in the current buffer. All other sections are descendants of this section. The value of this variable is set by **magit-insert-section** and you should never modify it.

For diff related sections a few additional tools exist.

`magit-diff-type` **&optional** *section*   [Function]
> Return the diff type of SECTION.
>
> The returned type is one of the symbols `staged`, `unstaged`, `committed`, or `undefined`. This type serves a similar purpose as the general type common to all sections (which is stored in the `type` slot of the corresponding `magit-section` struct) but takes additional information into account. When the SECTION isn't related to diffs and the buffer containing it also isn't a diff-only buffer, then return nil.
>
> Currently the type can also be one of `tracked` and `untracked`, but these values are not handled explicitly in every place they should be. A possible fix could be to just return nil here.
>
> The section has to be a `diff` or `hunk` section, or a section whose children are of type `diff`. If optional SECTION is nil, return the diff type for the current section. In buffers whose major mode is `magit-diff-mode` SECTION is ignored and the type is determined using other means. In `magit-revision-mode` buffers the type is always `committed`.

`magit-diff-scope` **&optional** *section strict*   [Function]
> Return the diff scope of SECTION or the selected section(s).
>
> A diff's "scope" describes what part of a diff is selected, it is a symbol, one of `region`, `hunk`, `hunks`, `file`, `files`, or `list`. Do not confuse this with the diff "type", as returned by `magit-diff-type`.
>
> If optional SECTION is non-nil, then return the scope of that, ignoring the sections selected by the region. Otherwise return the scope of the current section, or if the region is active and selects a valid group of diff related sections, the type of these sections, i.e. `hunks` or `files`. If SECTION (or if the current section that is nil) is a `hunk` section and the region starts and ends inside the body of a that section, then the type is `region`.
>
> If optional STRICT is non-nil then return nil if the diff type of the section at point is `untracked` or the section at point is not actually a `diff` but a `diffstat` section.

10.3 Refreshing buffers

All commands that create a new Magit buffer or change what is being displayed in an existing buffer do so by calling `magit-mode-setup`. Among other things, that function sets the buffer local values of `default-directory` (to the top-level of the repository), `magit-refresh-function`, and `magit-refresh-args`.

Buffers are refreshed by calling the function that is the local value of `magit-refresh-function` (a function named `magit-*-refresh-buffer`, where * may be something like `diff`) with the value of `magit-refresh-args` as arguments.

`magit-mode-setup` *buffer switch-func mode refresh-func* **&optional**   [Macro]
> *refresh-args*
> This function displays and selects BUFFER, turns on MODE, and refreshes a first time.
>
> This function displays and optionally selects BUFFER by calling `magit-mode-display-buffer` with BUFFER, MODE and SWITCH-FUNC as arguments. Then

it sets the local value of `magit-refresh-function` to REFRESH-FUNC and that of `magit-refresh-args` to REFRESH-ARGS. Finally it creates the buffer content by calling REFRESH-FUNC with REFRESH-ARGS as arguments.

All arguments are evaluated before switching to BUFFER.

`magit-mode-display-buffer` *buffer mode* **&optional** *switch-function*   [Function]
> This function display BUFFER in some window and select it. BUFFER may be a buffer or a string, the name of a buffer. The buffer is returned.
>
> Unless BUFFER is already displayed in the selected frame, store the previous window configuration as a buffer local value, so that it can later be restored by `magit-mode-bury-buffer`.
>
> The buffer is displayed and selected using SWITCH-FUNCTION. If that is `nil` then `pop-to-buffer` is used if the current buffer's major mode derives from `magit-mode`. Otherwise `switch-to-buffer` is used.

`magit-refresh-function`   [Variable]
> The value of this buffer-local variable is the function used to refresh the current buffer. It is called with `magit-refresh-args` as arguments.

`magit-refresh-args`   [Variable]
> The list of arguments used by `magit-refresh-function` to refresh the current buffer. `magit-refresh-function` is called with these arguments.
>
> The value is usually set using `magit-mode-setup`, but in some cases it's also useful to provide commands which can change the value. For example, the `magit-diff-refresh-popup` can be used to change any of the arguments used to display the diff, without having to specify again which differences should be shown. `magit-diff-more-context`, `magit-diff-less-context`, and `magit-diff-default-context` change just the -U<N> argument. In both case this is done by changing the value of this variable and then calling this `magit-refresh-function`.

10.4 Conventions

10.4.1 Confirmation and completion

Dangerous operations that may lead to data loss have to be confirmed by default. With a multi-section selection, this is done using questions that can be answered with "yes" or "no". When the region isn't active, or if it doesn't constitute a valid section selection, then such commands instead read a single item in the minibuffer. When the value of the current section is among the possible choices, then that is presented as default choice. To confirm the action on a single item, the user has to answer RET (instead of "yes"), and to abort, C-g (instead of "no"). But alternatively the user may also select another item, just like if the command had been invoked with no suitable section at point at all.

10.4.2 Theming Faces

The default theme uses blue for local branches, green for remote branches, and goldenrod (brownish yellow) for tags. When creating a new theme, you should probably follow that example. If your theme already uses other colors, then stick to that.

In older releases these reference faces used to have a background color and a box around them. The basic default faces no longer do so, to make Magit buffers much less noisy, and you should follow that example at least with regards to boxes. (Boxes were used in the past to work around a conflict between the highlighting overlay and text property backgrounds. That's no longer necessary because highlighting no longer causes other background colors to disappear.) Alternatively you can keep the background color and/or box, but then have to take special care to adjust `magit-branch-current` accordingly. By default it looks mostly like `magit-branch-local`, but with a box (by default the former is the only face that uses a box, exactly so that it sticks out). If the former also uses a box, then you have to make sure that it differs in some other way from the latter.

The most difficult faces to theme are those related to diffs, headings, highlighting, and the region. There are faces that fall into all four groups - expect to spend some time getting this right.

The `region` face in the default theme, in both the light and dark variants, as well as in many other themes, distributed with Emacs or by third-parties, is very ugly. It is common to use a background color that really sticks out, which is ugly but if that were the only problem then it would be acceptable. Unfortunately many themes also set the foreground color, which ensures that all text within the region is readable. Without doing that there might be cases where some foreground color is too close to the region background color to still be readable. But it also means that text within the region loses all syntax highlighting.

I consider the work that went into getting the `region` face right to be a good indicator for the general quality of a theme. My recommendation for the `region` face is this: use a background color slightly different from the background color of the `default` face, and do not set the foreground color at all. So for a light theme you might use a light (possibly tinted) gray as the background color of `default` and a somewhat darker gray for the background of `region`. That should usually be enough to not collide with the foreground color of any other face. But if some other faces also set a light gray as background color, then you should also make sure it doesn't collide with those (in some cases it might be acceptable though).

Magit only uses the `region` face when the region is "invalid" by its own definition. In a Magit buffer the region is used to either select multiple sibling sections, so that commands which support it act on all of these sections instead of just the current section, or to select lines within a single hunk section. In all other cases, the section is considered invalid and Magit won't act on it. But such invalid sections happen, either because the user has not moved point enough yet to make it valid or because she wants to use a non-magit command to act on the region, e.g. `kill-region`.

So using the regular `region` face for invalid sections is a feature. It tells the user that Magit won't be able to act on it. It's acceptable if that face looks a bit odd and even (but less so) if it collides with the background colors of section headings and other things that have a background color.

Magit highlights the current section. If a section has subsections, then all of them are highlighted. This is done using faces that have "highlight" in their names. For most sections, `magit-section-highlight` is used for both the body and the heading. Like the `region` face, it should only set the background color to something similar to that of `default`. The highlight background color must be different from both the `region` background color and the `default` background color.

For diff related sections Magit uses various faces to highlight different parts of the selected section(s). Note that hunk headings, unlike all other section headings, by default have a background color, because it is useful to have very visible separators between hunks. That face `magit-diff-hunk-heading`, should be different from both `magit-diff-hunk-heading-highlight` and `magit-section-highlight`, as well as from `magit-diff-context` and `magit-diff-context-highlight`. By default we do that by changing the foreground color. Changing the background color would lead to complications, and there are already enough we cannot get around. (Also note that it is generally a good idea for section headings to always be bold, but only for sections that have subsections).

When there is a valid region selecting diff-related sibling sections, i.e. multiple files or hunks, then the bodies of all these sections use the respective highlight faces, but additionally the headings instead use one of the faces `magit-diff-file-heading-selection` or `magit-diff-hunk-heading-selection`. These faces have to be different from the regular highlight variants to provide explicit visual indication that the region is active.

When theming diff related faces, start by setting the option `magit-diff-refine-hunk` to `all`. You might personally prefer to only refine the current hunk or not use hunk refinement at all, but some of the users of your theme want all hunks to be refined, so you have to cater to that.

(Also turn on `magit-diff-highlight-indentation`, `magit-diff-highlight-trailing`, and `magit-diff-paint-whitespace`; and insert some whitespace errors into the code you use for testing.)

For e.g. "added lines" you have to adjust three faces: `magit-diff-added`, `magit-diff-added-highlight`, and `smerge-refined-added`. Make sure that the latter works well with both of the former, as well as `smerge-other` and `diff-added`. Then do the same for the removed lines, context lines, lines added by us, and lines added by them. Also make sure the respective added, removed, and context faces use approximately the same saturation for both the highlighted and unhighlighted variants. Also make sure the file and diff headings work nicely with context lines (e.g. make them look different). Line faces should set both the foreground and the background color. For example, for added lines use two different greens.

It's best if the foreground color of both the highlighted and the unhighlighted variants are the same, so you will need to have to find a color that works well on the highlight and unhighlighted background, the refine background, and the highlight context background. When there is an hunk internal region, then the added- and removed-lines background color is used only within that region. Outside the region the highlighted context background color is used. This makes it easier to see what is being staged. With an hunk internal region the hunk heading is shown using `magit-diff-hunk-heading-selection`, and so are the thin lines that are added around the lines that fall within the region. The background color of that has to be distinct enough from the various other involved background colors.

Nobody said this would be easy. If your theme restricts itself to a certain set of colors, then you should make an exception here. Otherwise it would be impossible to make the diffs look good in each and every variation. Actually you might want to just stick to the default definitions for these faces. You have been warned. Also please note that if you do not get this right, this will in some cases look to users like bugs in Magit - so please do it right or not at all.

Appendix A   FAQ

Below you find a list of frequently asked questions. For a list of frequently **and recently** asked questions, i.e. questions that haven't made it into the manual yet, see `https://github.com/magit/magit/wiki/FAQ`.

A.1 Magit is slow

See Section 9.2.2 [Performance], page 56.

A.2 I am having problems committing

That likely means that Magit is having problems finding an appropriate emacsclient executable. See Section "Configuring With-Editor" in `with-editor` and Section "Debugging" in `with-editor`.

A.3 I am using an Emacs release older than 24.4

At least version 24.4 is required. There is no way around it.

If you own the machine you work on, then consider updating to the latest release provided by your distribution. If it doesn't feature a recent enough release, then you will have to use a backport package or build Emacs from source.

Installing Emacs from source is quite simple. See the instructions at `http://git.savannah.gnu.org/cgit/emacs.git/tree/INSTALL` and `http://git.savannah.gnu.org/cgit/emacs.git/tree/INSTALL.REPO` to get an idea of that this involves. But when you perform the installation then use the instructions for the release you are actually installing.

Unfortunately these instructions do not cover the hardest part (which is the hardest part exactly because it is not covered there): installing the build time dependencies.

For that you'll need to perform a web search and find an appropriate tutorial for your distribution. If you think you should not have had to do that yourself, then consider informing me about the resources that helped you figure what to do for your specific setup, so that I can post a link here. That way those coming after you have it easier.

A.4 I am using a Git release older than 1.9.4

At least version 1.9.4 is required. There is no way around it.

If you own the machine, then consider updating to the latest release provided by your distribution. If it doesn't feature a recent enough release, then you will have to use a backport package or build Git from source.

Installing Git from source is quite simple. See the instructions at `https://github.com/git/git/blob/master/INSTALL` to get an idea of that this involves. But when you perform the installation then use the instructions for the release you are actually installing.

A.5 I am using MS Windows and cannot push with Magit

It's almost certain that Magit is only incidental to this issue. It is much more likely that this is a configuration issue, even if you can push on the command line.

Detailed setup instructions can be found at `https://github.com/magit/magit/wiki/Pushing-with-Magit-from-Windows`.

A.6 How to install the gitman info manual?

Git's manpages can be exported as an info manual called `gitman`. Magit's own info manual links to nodes in that manual instead of the actual manpages because texinfo sadly doesn't support linking to manpages.

Unfortunately many distributions do not install the `gitman` manual by default. Some distributions may provide a separate package containing the info manual. Please let me know the name of that package for your distribution, so that I can mention here.

If the distribution you are using does not offer a package that contains the `gitman` manual, then you have to install it manually. Clone Git's own Git repository, checkout the tag corresponding to the Git release you have installed, and follow the instructions in `INSTALL`. The relevant make targets are `info` and `install-info`.

Alternatively you may add this advice to your `init.el` file.

```
(defadvice Info-follow-nearest-node (around gitman activate)
  "When encountering a cross reference to the 'gitman' info
manual, then instead of following that cross reference show
the actual manpage using the function 'man'."
  (let ((node (Info-get-token
               (point) "\\*note[ \n\t]+"
               "\\*note[ \n\t]+\\(([^:]*\\)):\\(:\\|[ \n\t]*(\\))?")))
    (if (and node (string-match "^(gitman)\\(.+\\)" node))
        (progn (require 'man)
               (man (match-string 1 node)))
      ad-do-it)))
```

Or if you are using MS Windows and `man` is not available, use this variation with used the Emacs Lisp implementation provided by the `woman` package.

```
(defadvice Info-follow-nearest-node (around gitman activate)
  "When encountering a cross reference to the 'gitman' info
manual, then instead of following that cross reference show
the actual manpage using the function 'woman'."
  (let ((node (Info-get-token
               (point) "\\*note[ \n\t]+"
               "\\*note[ \n\t]+\\(([^:]*\\)):\\(:\\|[ \n\t]*(\\))?")))
    (if (and node (string-match "^(gitman)\\(.+\\)" node))
        (progn (require 'woman)
               (woman (match-string 1 node)))
      ad-do-it)))
```

Did I mention that texinfo cross reference are just awful? (This is just one of many issues.)

A.7 How can I show Git's output?

To show the output of recently run git commands, press $ (or, if that isn't available, M-x magit-process-buffer). This will show a buffer containing a section per git invocation; as always press TAB to expand or collapse them.

By default git's output is only inserted into the process buffer if it is run for side-effects. When the output is consumed in some way then also inserting it into the process buffer would be to expensive. For debugging purposes it's possible to do so anyway by setting magit-git-debug to t.

A.8 Expanding a file to show the diff causes it to disappear

This is probably caused by a change of a diff.* Git variable. You probably set that variable for a reason, and should therefore only undo that setting in Magit by customizing magit-git-global-arguments.

A.9 Magit claims repository accessed using Tramp does not exist

"There is no Git repository in /ssh:host:/path/to/repository".

Magit requires at least version 1.9.4. When connecting to a remote machine using Tramp it requires that same version on that remote.

By default Tramp searches for programs in the directories given by the output of getconf PATH on the remote host. Therefore, if the remote git version that you intend to use lives in a non-standard location, you may need to alter tramp-remote-path. Consult the Tramp documentation on remote programs http://www.gnu.org/software/emacs/manual/html_node/tramp/Remote-Programs.html for details.

There are others reasons why Magit/Git might think that there is no repository where there actually is one, but when this is being reported then it's usually the above.

A.10 Can Magit be used as ediff-version-control-package?

No, it cannot. For that to work the functions ediff-magit-internal and ediff-magit-merge-internal would have to be implemented, and they are not. These two functions are only used by the three commands ediff-revision, ediff-merge-revisions-with-ancestor, and ediff-merge-revisions.

These commands only delegate the task of populating buffers with certain revisions to the "internal" functions. The equally important task of determining which revisions are to be compared/merged is not delegated. Instead this is done without any support whatsoever, from the version control package/system - meaning that the user has to enter the revisions explicitly. Instead of implementing ediff-magit-internal we provide magit-ediff-compare, which handles both tasks like it is 2005.

The other commands ediff-merge-revisions and ediff-merge-revisions-with-ancestor are normally not what you want when using a modern version control system like Git. Instead of letting the user resolve only those conflicts which Git could not resolve on its own, they throw away all work done by Git and then expect the user to manually merge all conflicts, including those that had already been resolved. That made sense back in the days when version control systems couldn't merge (or so I have been told), but not anymore. Once in a blue moon you might actually want to see all conflicts, in which case you **can** use these commands, which then use `ediff-vc-merge-internal`. So we don't actually have to implement `ediff-magit-merge-internal`. Instead we provide the more useful command `magit-ediff-resolve` which only shows yet-to-be resolved conflicts.

A.11 How to show diffs for gpg-encrypted files?

Git supports showing diffs for encrypted files, but has to be told to do so. Since Magit just uses Git to get the diffs, configuring Git also affects the diffs displayed inside Magit.

```
git config --global diff.gpg.textconv "gpg --no-tty --decrypt"
echo "*.gpg filter=gpg diff=gpg" > .gitattributes
```

A.12 Emacs 24.5 hangs when loading Magit

This is actually triggered by loading Tramp. See https://debbugs.gnu.org/cgi/bugreport.cgi?bug~20015 for details. You can work around the problem by setting `tramp-ssh-controlmaster-options`. Changing your DNS server (e.g. to Google's 8.8.8.8) may also be sufficient to work around the issue.

Appendix B Keystroke Index

Appendix C Command Index

S

W

Appendix D Function Index

Appendix E Variable Index